I0764726

Christian Book Marketing 2026

Published by Glorybound Publishing, Camp Verde, AZ
SAN 256-4564
1st Ed
Printed in the United States of America
ISBN 978-1-60789-269-4 1-60789-269-3
Library of Congress Cataloging-in-Publication data is available on file.
Hauser, Sheri, 1957-

Christian Book Marketing 2026/Sheri Hauser
Includes biographical reference.

1. Business 2. Self-help

I. Title

www.gloryboundpublishing.com
www.bookmarketmania.com
www.sherihauser.com

Christian Book Marketing 2026

by Sheri Hauser
Alison Kovaleski - Editor

Glorybound Publishing
Camp Verde, AZ
in the year 2026

Christian Book Marketing 2026

The purpose of this book is to help authors clarify their goals and set a realistic path for book sales in 2026.

Credentials of the Author:

Sheri Hauser is the owner of Glorybound Publishing, which she founded in 2005 with the release of her own series of books. She went to the University of Las Vegas to study Photoshop and became a webmaster. She has been working with Adobe software—mainly InDesign—since its earliest versions. It is the premier pagination software, which makes it perfect for compiling manuscripts into books. InDesign coordinates seamlessly with Photoshop, Illustrator, Professional Acrobat and Epub to provide a foundation that can handle any type of book.

Glorybound has published over 800 books as of 2026—some as large as 365 pages containing 354 photos. In 2022, Sheri obtained a diploma in Sound Engineering and opened a sound studio in her office for the purpose of releasing audiobooks on ACX. In 2023, she earned a diploma in Social Media Marketing and launched out on a small business website, Alignable, to practice. She was named Small Business of the Year for two years in a row, and then in 2024 joined other esteemed Alignable businesses in the Top 50 Businesses of Alignable. Over the past decade, she has served on several boards, including Archaeology, OLLI, Friends of the Library, and the Chamber of Commerce. It is also noteworthy that her gingerbread house received the highest award at the Camp Verde, Arizona Christmas festival in 2025. ☺

This background information is provided to demonstrate Sheri's qualifications and knowledge on how to sell books. She hopes you find this book helpful….and if you do, please give her a recommendation!

Table of Contents

Introduction →

Sales vs. Exposure

The difference with Christian books is that we do not promote sales, but promote exposure… Show and Tell. The goal is not to make money, but to share well-written, newly released Christian material.

Consider: Does making money demonstrate the success of a business? When you write a book, it is like going into business. You have a product and provide a way for others to purchase it. The success is based on the number of sales. This is an important principle to understand when dealing with Christian authors because their primary motivation is not sales, so often they are negligent in promoting their books. Take a look at Jesus and the promotion of the Gospel. How did He promote it? I would say that He promoted it by showing it was true…Show and Tell. He told many His message, and because the words were alive, the message continued to speak for itself.

The main difference with Christian writing is that it is based on the Living Word, or Rhema Word. God did not stop talking when the Bible as we know it was canonized. He continues to breathe today through the power of the Holy Spirit. In essence, a Christian book penned by someone prompted by the Holy Spirit has a voice of its own; it will continue to speak for itself because the words are alive.

So, did Jesus market the Gospel? You betcha. And in the end, there were huge sales. The Bible continues to be the book with the largest sales of any other book in the world. But the goal wasn't sales of Bibles—but changed lives. When I initially began compiling books, I put together many for free. I told Christian authors, "I will put a book together for free if it will change lives; and sometimes the only life changed is the author's life when he/she is given the information used to write the book."

As Christian authors, our success is measured in the number of changed lives. Is one changed more than another? Sure. So, we have no true measuring stick except seeing the difference in someone after they read your book.

I have diligently reviewed conventional marketing options. Many of these fail with Christian titles because shoppers look to be entertained rather than to have their lives changed. And, even within the religious sector, many are divided, limiting their reading to specific authors, etc. There are churches which control the reading of the congregation, like mixing the feed for an exotic zoo animal. They realize that words have power. And indeed, they do. That is why Christian authors write… remember.

Firstly, let's look at the aspects of conventional book marketing, then we will pull it around to settle on what will genuinely work for Christian books.

Onward→

Christian Book Marketing 2026

Section 1 →

General Book Marketing

The Process of Marketing

The process of marketing a *top seller* begins with inception of the book. A manuscript is written, edited, and compiled using pagination software to format it to the appropriate size for the best user experience. For example, a cookbook should be large enough to stay open, while a hiking trail book should be small enough to carry. A hiker does not want to carry around a laminated hardbound book.

- A release date of the book is set.
- The marketing agency obtains ARCs (advance reader copies) prior to the release date of the book. These copies are specifically for distribution to create hype in anticipation of the book's release. These may be E-books or bound copies.
- Make a Press Release. It is a single sheet with a photo of the author, a summary of the book, where it is distributed, the book cover, and how to contact the author. A general press release can serve as an introduction to events or as a request to book outlets. (See sample in section 6.)
- Promotional events are scheduled.
- Book signing at a library, bookstore, grocery store, or any place willing to become an outlet for book sales.
- Podcast
- Live interview at a radio station or television channel
- May be in conjunction with a community event. Put up a special tent and allow individuals to personally meet the author.

- Begin gathering book reviews. Book reviews [on Amazon] are a powerful way to gain traction within the sales matrix. Reviews provide reader credibility with the goal of converting visitors into buyers.

Endorsements and Reviews

Endorsements are a powerful tool that you can use *before* your book has been released. To earn an endorsement, you can send an ARC or copy of your manuscript (finished or unfinished) to a notable name in the field your book represents. If this person is willing, they can write a short review of your book and send it back to you. This is especially useful for non-fiction or business books, because it lends authority to your book right from the word "go." You can take quotes from the review and include them on your cover design as an immediate representation of the quality of your book.

Trade Reviews are penned by established publishing industry professionals. Trade reviews have become an industry within an industry, since there are quite a few companies that are dedicated to the service. The heaviest hitters in this category are **Publishers Weekly** and **Kirkus Reviews**. **Blue Ink Review** is another popular choice, as they specialize in self-published/independent books. There are two slight downsides to trade reviews: first, they charge a fee in order to review your book, and second, there is no guarantee that it will be a positive review. However, these are respected voices within the publishing industry. If you plan to market your book to retail distributors such as Barnes & Noble and Tattered Cover, or if you would like to see your book in the local library, trade reviews are a good place to start.

Reader Reviews are provided by individuals who purchased your book and left a review of it online. These can either be positive or negative, and can come from anyone. The most common places to find them are either on the Amazon page where your book is listed or on **Goodreads**. Reader reviews are trickier than they sound. Amazon has extremely strict guidelines regarding which reviews are accepted. These policies are intended to keep reviews as honest as possible. The good news is that Goodreads does not seem to have the same stringent policies. It is a fun website where friends can follow each other's reading-progress and book reviews. It does seem to be more focused on fiction, but non-fiction books make an appearance, too.

An Editorial Review is when a third-party, professional entity reviews your book. This is typically in an article or a blog. The term can sometimes be used interchangeably with a trade review, but in this case, we are using it to denote an entity that does not solely provide publishing services. An editorial review can come from a local blogger, news station, or The New York Times. Some authors consider it "hitting the big time" if a review of their book appears in The New York Times. There are plenty of bloggers out there who would be more than delighted to post a review of your book. Like trade reviews, they can either be paid or free. Before requesting that your book be reviewed by a blogger, be sure to look through their website to determine the size and demographics of their audience. You will want to make sure their readership aligns with your target audience and consists of the readers who are most likely to buy your book. If you actively pursue editorial reviews, you can earn them with the same laser-focus as an endorsement. But, as always, be prepared for the possibility of a negative review.

https://www.linkedin.com/pulse/4-types-book-reviews-my-word-publishing-1

Good Book Reviews

Answer from AI

Key elements of a good book review

- **Introduction:** Briefly introduce the book title, author, and the main theme. State your overall opinion up front.
- **Summary:** Provide a short, spoiler-free overview of the plot and its primary purpose or audience.
- **Analysis:** Discuss specific aspects you liked or disliked, such as characters, writing style, plot structure, or themes. Use specific examples from the book to support your points.
- **Personal Reflection:** Share your personal reaction to the book.
- **Conclusion:** Give a final summary of your thoughts and a recommendation, explaining who might enjoy the book.

Samples of good book reviews:

What must a book review contain?

Like all works of art, no two book reviews will be identical. But fear not: there are a few guidelines for any aspiring book reviewer to follow. Most book reviews, for instance, are less than 1,500 words long, with the sweet spot hitting somewhere around the 1,000-word mark. (However, this may vary depending on the platform on which you're writing, as we'll see later.)

In addition, all reviews share some universal elements, as shown in our book review templates. These include:

- A review will offer a concise plot summary of the book.
- A book review will offer an evaluation of the work.
- A book review will offer a recommendation for the audience.

What are the three main parts of a book review?

We covered this in detail (with the help of some stellar examples) in our post on how to write a book review, but basically, these are the three crucial elements you should know:

The summary covers the premise of the book and its central theme, so readers can understand what you're referring to in the rest of your review. This means that, if a person hasn't read the book, they can go through the summary to get a quick idea of what it's about. (As such, there should be no spoilers!)

The analysis is where, if it's a fiction book, you talk more about the book, its plot, theme, and characters. If it's nonfiction, you have to consider whether the book effectively achieves what it set out to do.

The recommendation is where your personal opinion comes in the strongest, and you give a verdict as to who you think might enjoy this book.

You can choose to be brief or detailed, depending on the kind of review you're writing, but you should always aim to cover these three points.

Which additional details can you include?

Once you've nailed down the basics, you can jazz things up a little and add some personal flavor to your book review by considering some of these elements:

- A star-rating (the default is five stars, but you can create your own scales);
- A bullet-point pros and cons list;
- Your favorite quotation from the book;
- Commentary on the format you read (e.g., e-book, print, or audiobook);
- Fun facts about the book or author;
- Other titles you think are similar.

https://reedsy.com/discovery/blog/book-review-examples

Research the best outlets for the book and begin to make connections with them to sell the book.

Books that are released on multiple platforms do best. Consider paperback, Kindle e-book, and audiobook. A book may be uploaded to IngramsSpark for distribution to the wholesale market and Kindle Direct Publishing (KDP) for direct retail sales.

How I Write Book Reviews

A book review needs to be somewhere between, "Great book!" and two pages of writing. Generally I write a book review using three sentences. The first sentence provides a draw to lure the audience in.

Examples can include:

- I couldn't put the book down
- Authors' best work yet
- Kept me on the edge of my chair
- Great contribution to literature

The next sentence indicates that I have read the book. It provides the 'meat' for the review. Ivorymind is an AI summarizer (among other things) https://app.ivorymind.com/

A book (files) can be uploaded in several formats and a short summary is generated upon request. I will put the short summary to this book below.

Christian Book Marketing 2026 summary

Christian books prioritize exposure and sharing well-written material over sales. The primary goal for many Christian authors is not profit but the impact their work can have on readers' lives. This perspective aligns with Jesus' approach to promoting the Gospel through authentic messaging rather than traditional marketing strategies. The essence of Christian writing is rooted in the Living Word, propelled by the Holy Spirit, which enables these works to resonate deeply and affect change. While commercial success can be measured by sales, the true measure of a Christian book's success lies in the transformation it inspires in its readers. Typical marketing tactics may not effectively reach audiences seeking spiritual growth, as many readers focus on entertainment rather than meaningful engagement. Consequently, a tailored strategy that emphasizes the life-changing power of Christian literature is essential for its success.

The final element to a well written book review is what I call, "Connect the flesh to the work."

A book is only as good as it is to the reader. If a reader provides a genuine connection to the book it becomes a testimony. Imagine that?

Let's practice making awesome book reviews....

1. One of the best resources for Christian book marketing I have read all year. The author's perspective aligns with Jesus' approach to promoting the Gospel through authentic messaging rather than traditional marketing strategies pulling in current marketing information. I will refer it to my friends. Five stars.

2. I can't wait to get started using these marketing strategies. The writer understands that while commercial success can be measured by sales, the true measure of a Christian book's success lies in the transformation it inspires in its readers. I am looking forward to greater success with the sales of my books following many of her strategies.

3. It is refreshing to see someone with marketing skills who understands Christian books. Typical marketing tactics may not effectively reach audiences seeking spiritual growth, as many readers focus on entertainment rather than meaningful engagement. I am going to look for her other marketing books. Great read!

In each of the sample book reviews above there is a lure followed by copying one of the points taken directly from the Ivorymind summary capped with a personal connection to the book.

Christian Book Marketing 2026

Section 1 General Book Marketing
Section 2 Selling Christian Books
- Knowledge Advantage
- What is the Goal for Your Book?
- Microphones in Publishing
- Amazon Book Ranking
- Utilize Search Words
- Book Clean-up
- Kindle E-Books on KDP
- Kindle Unlimited
- Author Central
- Author Website

Section 3 Target Marketing
Section 4 Avenues of Marketing
Section 5 Recognizing a Marketing Scam
Section 6 Book Reviews
Section 7 Selling Used Books
Section 8 Book Awards
Section 9 Develop a Book Launch Plan

Section 2 →

Selling Christian Books

Knowledge Advantage

> One of my favorite verses is from the Old Testament. It says, "*You stumble day and night, and the prophets stumble with you. So I will destroy your mother--my people are destroyed from the lack of knowledge*" (Hosea 4:5-6).

Knowledge is defined as facts, information, and skills acquired by a person through experience or education; the theoretical or practical understanding of a subject—an awareness or familiarity gained by experience of a fact or situation.

It seems to me that, as Christians, we have an advantage over all the rest of the authors because we have the opportunity to gain knowledge as well as insight from God on a topic. For certainly, with both we can go far.

Last week I had a dream. I will tell the dream with its interpretation because it brings *understanding* to the topic.

The dream:

A guy comes to my stepfather with something to sell him, which is fake. My stepfather takes out a gun and shoots the salesman in the eye. I am standing between the two of them and run away quickly to separate myself from the incident. I am afraid I will be tagged as a shooter as well because I am his daughter. The whole thing is too messy for me. I want no part of it.

Interpretation of the dream:

My stepfather was my mother's last husband (she had several), and I loved him dearly. He took care of her until she passed away from breast cancer at a young age. He spent all of their retirement savings and ended up living in poverty for several years beyond her death. He never remarried. I cared for him in his later years. He was a successful mobile home salesman for many years. The dream shows a guy trying to give him something fake. Gil (my stepfather) shoots him in the eye. After doing an extensive study of conventional book marketing, it is all about convincing others to buy your book—no matter what. It is self-absorbed; all about "I."

All of the book marketing techniques outlined above seek to elevate the book, make it look important or essential, and give it value so the customer is willing to spend money purchasing it. In the dream, Gil is a symbol of selfless sales. In essence, he was sold out to doing what was right, rather than promoting fake products to pad his pockets. Gil was more of a father to me than my biological father, so I stand between him and this other guy. The other guy represents false promotion. The dream tells me that I have hidden from promotion, afraid of being blamed for promoting myself (I) instead of God. I have been hiding from conventional book promotion because I saw it as fake, perhaps promoting a poor book, ballooning the ego and padding the bank account of a writer.

Yet I have not followed the edict from Hosea 4:5-6, putting my head in the sand rather than being willing to grow in knowledge with understanding of Godly principles for book marketing.

I have published over 700 books. Many authors have several books or series of books. They are constantly requesting marketing. Up until recently, I have refused. When I discovered beloved authors seeking marketing services (and being taken advantage of), I began to dig into the principles of book marketing to figure out how to offer them. I had the dream above (and didn't figure it out for a while) until I had a second dream where I lost my phone and couldn't find it. I was really trucking down the book marketing trail! I opened 11 book marketing websites to help authors display and sell their books.

I have written several books on dreams and dream interpretation that had phones in them, so I realized immediately that what God was trying to tell me is I need to ask Him about it, rather than everyone else. I had lost my connection to Him. You know the verse… "*Call out to me, and I will answer you — I will tell you great things, hidden things of which you are unaware*" (Jeremiah 33:3).

I was leaving out the other side of the equation in Hosea 4:5-6. Look at the New Testament…"*Now about food sacrificed to idols, we know that we all have knowledge [concerning this]. Knowledge [alone] makes [people self-righteously] arrogant, but love [that unselfishly seeks the best for others] builds up and encourages others to grow [in wisdom]*" (Amplified Bible, I Corinthians 8:1).

Paul is writing to the church in Corinth, which was afraid of eating food sacrificed to idols. They were afraid to mix what was socially OK with Godly principles. Ah! Sounds familiar.

The last dream tells me to ask God for insight into what is right to help with Christian book marketing, as stated in I John 4:1 and 4:6 … "*…do not believe every spirit, but test the spirits to see whether they are from God... We are from God. ... By this we know the Spirit of truth and the spirit of error.*"

So, I found my phone (my God line) and asked Him about book marketing from a Christian standpoint. Guess what? I came BACK to a bunch of stuff that He had told me when I released my first book in 2005!

Again…to take it from the start of this section…
Standard book marketing is self-promotion. The goal is getting the book (and the writer) in front of as large an audience as possible with hype (interviews, podcasts, Facebook posts, book awards), jockeying for a coveted position on Amazon pages with five-star book reviews and lots of book sales. Don't be tricked into believing the person is promoting the book, not themselves, because it is nearly impossible to sell a book with a pen name. The audience needs to associate the author with the book because it promotes validity.

The difference with a Christian author and their book is the goal. The primary goal of conventional book marketing is to make money. If an author does not have a goal of making money, then why bother with marketing at all?

What is the Goal for Your Book?

I contend that all authors must realize their goal for the book. What is your goal in doing what you did? Many tell me, "God downloaded this information, and I am being obedient to God in releasing it."

They are telling me they do not have a goal—but have fulfilled their goal, which was to please God by fulfilling His request. So, in essence, they throw it out there, declaring, "It's God's responsibility to do the marketing. He will bring whomever He wants to read it."

I asked AI the question, "How many books are on Amazon?"
Here is the answer, "Amazon has tens of millions of book titles available globally, with one source citing over 44 million, and another stating over 32.8 million published titles."

Suffice it to say, there are a lot of books on Amazon. There are 70,000 devotionals (alone) on Amazon. People find books on Amazon by typing in a string of words.

Example: devotionals for women. Searchers are sent to a page (which has 24 books on my desktop). Those looking for a book rarely drill down beyond 14 pages on the subject. Therefore, the coveted positions (which actually make the most sales) are in the first five pages. Amazon has a marketing matrix they put books into that figures out the book's standing on the search pages of the subject. There are many ways to increase a book's standing on Amazon pages—and that is a main feature of book marketing.

So, let's say you are an awesome Christian and God begins to speak to your soul about a topic, prompting you to write a book. You figure out how to edit and publish it by uploading it to KDP or IngramsSpark. If you do nothing further, the book will be posted on the last pages of the search under its topic. Let's see… perhaps it is a devotional. There are 70,000 devotionals with 24 per page. Your book will end up on page 2,916. Hmm.

But, you say, "Am I helping God out by doing some marketing? Can't He do whatever He wants? He could write the title of the book in the sky if He wants."

Sure…God is God. But, … "we are Christ's ambassadors; God is making his appeal through us. We speak for Christ when we plead, Come back to God!" (I Corinthians 5:20)

The Christian life is a cooperation between God and us. He has no physical body, so we are the hands of God reaching out to the world on behalf of Him. Does He need us? Yes. Otherwise, there would be no need for preaching the gospel or for missionaries to go abroad.

I think the problem comes in when the believer receives what he thinks is a message from God and writes it down but doesn't go back to God to figure out the rest of the instructions. It is like starting out on a trail. You seek direction from the trail guide and say, "I will take it from here. I got this." Then, you hike on down the trail. But what if you come to a fork in the trail? Do you stop, turn around, or just pick an arbitrary direction?

God didn't stop talking because we stopped listening. We can always return to Him for clarification and direction along the pathway.

In addition, consider the reason a preacher has a podium. Why does he have a microphone? Is he failing to trust God to deliver the message by going to the podium with a microphone? No, he has been entrusted with a message. Either he feels it is important to "get it out," or others are encouraging him to "be a voice to the congregation." He speaks (not THE voice of God), but an interpretation of the voice of God, which helps bring understanding to others.

Using methods to share the voice (which God has given in a book) is no different than a preacher using a podium and a microphone.

Consider:

- What options can be used as your microphone?
- How big of an audience are you trying to get the message to?
- Can the audience hear you?
- Can the audience understand you?

Microphones in Publishing

Options

Book events, ads, paid advertising on Amazon, podcasts, interviews, Facebook…and the same ones listed above under conventional book marketing.

Size of audience

Some promotions speak louder than others. Ask God which ones are for you and your book. A tent set up at a local event has a lower voice than a paid ad on Amazon.

Can they hear you?

Is your book up to the standards of professional editing and publishing? Should you do other languages, sizes, formats, an audiobook, Kindle e-book, put the book on the wholesale market, or the retail market? Can your audience hear you? If the person who needs your message cannot read, but is able to listen to an audiobook, then it is reasonable to make an audiobook. This is an extension of your podium or microphone.

Can they understand?

What God has told me is that books are similar to parking garages. People come into the book from varying levels of understanding, knowledge, etc. They can only come into the reading (of the book) from whatever level they are on. If the words and teaching are too complex for their level, they will not benefit from it. Many Christian books are written to fellow believers. I have seen manuscripts that use large words, incomplete scripture documentation, and lean on teaching bred from a specific interpretation of a religion.

If the writer is a Baptist, for example, he may assume the reader feels the same way he does about spiritual gifts and speaking in tongues. In essence, he has cut off the first floor of the parking garage for anyone who does not come from the same religious standing. All his readers come in above the second floor.

I will admit the writing in this book is second or third level—because it is written to a believer who has written and published a book and is contemplating marketing. I have not left a ground-floor option for thinking. To make the writing stronger, I need to add some basic groundwork—or information for those who have not yet written a book.

I am not advocating that all Christian books offer readers entry at the lowest level, but attempting to increase awareness that your book is written to a specific audience. Basic marketing teaches the importance of understanding who your audience is. Once you understand who the book is written for, then you will be able to figure out how to reach them where they are.

Here are some avenues to increase exposure. Again, ask God which ones are best for you and your book.

- Amazon Book Ranking
- Utilize Search Words
- Hashtags
- Google AI

Amazon Book Ranking

First, learn how Amazon ranks books on its pages. Consider the sales matrix used by Amazon—which books go on which pages. Why are some books on the first pages?

Paid Ads put books on the first pages. Search words are assigned click-value. When a person types in a word, Amazon sends him to your book (because it was set up by you in the Ad software), then once he clicks on the book, you are charged for the direction . Two books may have sponsored ads running for the same subject. The one with the highest click value will be shown first.

Sales numbers. High sales will get you on the front pages. Think of Amazon like a grocery store. They put the seasonal items on the end cap because they know people shop more for items that are on the end cap aisle. Amazon makes money when they sell your book. More sales = more money. Simple.

New books may show up on the first pages for a while.

Books with a lot of reviews demonstrate consumer trust. Verified Reviews rank higher than unverified reviews.

A unified show on Amazon helps. Does your book have robust search words? Is the cover snappy? Does your book point to a hot topic? Is Author Central filled out? Does your photo show up alongside the book? Have you applied for a unique URL? People will find you more easily if your name is part of the URL.

A book demonstrates versatility if several formats are offered. These include paperback, hardback, Kindle e-book, and an audiobook. I admit that not all books need these formats, but expanding them may help with exposure on Amazon.

Utilize Search Words

Amazon search words help readers locate the book. KDP permits seven search words or phrases. Find the most common phrases with the highest traffic for books similar to yours. KDP Rocket is a good resource.

Embed the copyright and add keywords (or metadata) into the book and book cover files before they are uploaded to KDP or IngramsSpark. InDesign or Photoshop (file> Document title, author name, rating, key words, copyright information) Adobe Professional Acrobat (Document Properties>description, key words)

KDP Rocket is book marketing software. I bought it for $100 some years back as a one-time purchase. It specifically assists with locating the best search words (metadata), similar books, seeing which books are selling and for how much. It is useful information for developing paid Amazon ads. The idea with KDP Rocket is words are worth money. People type in certain words or groups of words to look for subjects. Some words are typed in more often. And, to add to that information, some words that are typed into the search engine generate more sales than others. For instance, if you have a prayer book and enter the words *prayer book* into KDP Rocket, it will tell you how many searches per month are made for that phrase.

Then it will show who sells what books and the price of the books. The goal of using KDP Rocket is to locate niche topics for your book. Suppose the prayer book sample above is specific to praying for sons who are in military service. It may be better to add a key word group, such as *father's prayer for military son.* The topic has been narrowed down and the book is sure to show up on the first pages of a search for these specific words…but is anyone actually typing in THOSE words? Perhaps the words they are typing in are *prayers for military children.* KDP will tell you. A sure way to get your book on the top pages of a search on Amazon is to find niche topics with high search numbers and a low number of books that will compete with yours.

If you do not have KDP Rocket, you can do a similar search by writing down a list of words that your book represents. Open Amazon, specify books, and type each word or phrase into the search bar. Amazon will give groups of word lists, which are the first several words people are typing into their search bar. For instance, if you type in *prayers for military*…then Amazon will offer several suggestions on how to complete the sentence based on how many are searching for a similar topic. Those at the top of their list that most closely resemble your topic will be the best word groupings to use as your search words.

Hashtags

(source: https://www.facebook.com/help/587836257914341)

Hashtags turn topics and phrases into clickable links in your posts on your personal timeline, Page or groups. This helps people find posts about topics they're interested in. To make a hashtag, write # (the number sign) along with a topic or phrase and add it to your post. For example:

I just saw the cutest puppy! **#dogs**.

When you click a hashtag, you'll see a feed of posts that include that hashtag. You may also see some related hashtags at the top of the page.

Please keep in mind:

A hashtag must be written as a single word, without any spaces.

You can include numbers in a hashtag, but punctuation and special characters (like $ and %) won't work.

You can search for a hashtag using the search bar at the top of any page.

You'll only see posts that were shared with you.

Different Uses of Hashtags on Social Media
(source: https://blogs.mtu.edu/social-media/2022/05/16/usage-differences-in-hashtags-on-facebook-twitter-and-instagram-social/)

What is a hashtag?

A hashtag is a keyword or phrase begun by a hash symbol (#) (i.e., #MichiganTech #ThisIsTech #TomorrowNeeds). On social media, hashtags allow users to find posts relating to the specific hashtag.

How are hashtags used?

Hashtags are also used to draw attention to a social media post. On both Instagram and X/Twitter, it is not uncommon for users to follow a specific hashtag. An example would be how the main Michigan Tech Instagram account follows #MichiganTech because we want to be able to see posts relating to the University. We also follow #UpperPeninsula and #MTUBound.

When in doubt trying to decide on a hashtag, check out our MTU Hashtag list.

All in all, hashtags are necessary because they help people find your social media content.

X (formerly Twitter):

X/Twitter has a limited character amount per post/tweet; therefore, when using hashtags on this platform, it is important to be succinct.

Hashtag Recommendations for X/Twitter:

We recommend using one or two hashtags on a single tweet.

Only use hashtags when they are relevant to your tweet.

Look at the trending hashtags and if it makes sense to join in on the conversation, don't hesitate to use the hashtag in a tweet!

Facebook:

Facebook has grown and shifted—and hashtag usage on the platform has, too. There are key factors and best practices to consider when using hashtags in Facebook posts.

Users Cannot Follow a Hashtag on Facebook

Not being able to follow a hashtag on Facebook is one large reason why usage has gone down. On other platforms, such as X/Twitter and Instagram, a hashtag that a user follows will show up directly in their feed, giving them an incentive to follow hashtags. Facebook does not have this feature.

Limit Hashtag Usage

Research from the Pew Research Institute indicates that the fewer hashtags you use, the higher engagement you will receive on a post. Sticking to relevant hashtags can improve your content engagement.

Free hashtag apps like **Hashtag Expert**, **Hashtag Pro**, and **Trending Hashtags AI** help you find and generate trending hashtags for platforms like Instagram and TikTok. Other free tools, such as **RiteTag** and **QuillBot's AI Hashtag Generator,** offer suggestions based on keywords or images and provide analytics on hashtag performance.

Google AI

Free hashtag generator apps

Hashtag Expert: Uses AI to find trending hashtags based on a starting keyword, offers performance tracking, and organizes hashtags into collections. Available on the App Store and as a web tool, says Hashtag Expert.

Hashtag Pro: Generates over 40 hashtags from a single keyword for multiple social media platforms, including Instagram, TikTok, and YouTube.

Trending Hashtags AI: Finds and suggests trending hashtags, provides AI-powered suggestions, and tracks performance to help boost engagement. Available on Google Play.

Book Clean-up

Are there too many versions of your book?

One thing to keep in mind is that anyone can sell your book on Amazon. Initially, I was shocked to learn this. How is it possible, given that you have complete control (assuming it is released on KDP) of the printing and retail price?

The other day, an author stopped by my office, distraught, claiming that his book was being sold for $48.00 when we listed the retail price at $29.00. How is this possible?

Anyone can put books up for sale on Amazon through a program called Seller Central. In fact, libraries routinely sell off excess books donated to them and put them on Seller Central. When someone orders the book, Amazon sends an email, and it is fulfilled, either by directly mailing it to the customer (FBM, *Fulfillment by Merchant*) or it is shipped from the Amazon storage facility (FBA, *Fulfillment by Amazon).* Amazon makes money coming and going! When the merchant (the person with the book he wants to sell) signs up, Amazon handles the advertising billing for the service. If the book(s) are stored at an Amazon facility, they must be mailed to a specific place. The merchant is billed storage fees for as long as the books are stored there, pending sales. Seller Central is a good idea for those with a stack of conventionally printed books, because it offers an equal advertising option for them. The person purchasing the book often does not know where it came from, but is happy to get it at a good price.

Back to the question posed above, "How did his book get posted on Amazon for a different price than the one he put into KDP?"

The answer was found by clicking on the picture of the book. The right side of the screen lists who is selling it. A second-hand store was selling his book! The merchant lists whether the book is new or used, as both are sold through the program. This book had a list price of $48. Who knows whether the guy/gal had an actual book, or was treasure hunting when he listed it. It is a unique book, and he may have ventured to throw it out there, see if he can get some bites, and if someone orders, he will purchase it direct retail (from the KDP side of Amazon) for $29 and make a quick $19.

The other scenario is that the author gave free copies to someone and they were snagged by the second-hand book vendor. Some people also make money scanning book ISBNs using the software and scoop up valuable books to resell on Seller Central. Don't be surprised if your book is found in that scoop. Whenever I see an author who is upset about finding their book being sold by someone else, I encourage him/her by telling them that the person who is selling it must have thought it was valuable. Leave it alone.

KDP Home Page Clean-up

It is wise to un-publish books from your home page that are not useful for today. I have seen home pages where authors published an edition and then opened another edition (of the same book) that includes revisions. This is not the best option. Once a book is published (officially by KDP), it will be listed on Amazon. If the file is opened (by you) on the home page and not pushed through the tabs, it will remain in a partially published state (once again) and no one will be able to order the book. It will be presented as **Unavailable**.

If you restart the same book and publish it on Amazon, it will display both editions—with one being available and one not being available. People who are shopping for the book may stumble on the unavailable option of the book rather than the available one. So, just clean it up. Un-publish that old file. The easiest way to do it is to publish OVER the first file by uploading new files of the book and cover image. This will work unless you have substantially changed the size or page count to need a new cover.

Kindle E-Books on KDP

Kindle Books published on KDP have several ways to increase exposure.

Make sure the book looks good as an e-book. A common problem with the display of e-books is that certain fonts smash letters together, causing them to overlap. KDP does not have an e-book preview option, so I advise looking at it using the free software, *Adobe Digital Editions*. There are two types of e-books. Non-reflowable, or fixed layout (which is for books with pictures), and reflowable (which is for books without pictures). The first one will be read on a Kindle Reader device while the other one can be read on a cell phone. Remove any empty pages, do a table of contents (if you want—it is not required), and remove page numbers. A lot of the time, I put the cover on the first page and move the ISBN data to the back of the book because once the reader opens the book, the cover is not seen again. All links can be made active in InDesign under the Interactive Hyperlink tab. Make sure they work. There is nothing more frustrating than a broken link.

Kindle Create is the dedicated software app free download from Amazon which helps to make a nice e-book. Recently I began using this software and have had success with e-books.

The advantage of using Kindle Create is that it can be used to develop a clean highly searchable book with active links, a table of contents and Alt Text photos—and it's free. Essentially, it checks all the boxes for uploading a kindle e-book to KDP.

**Added note*. *If you have a large file (lots of photos and/or pages) it can be saved in Acrobat Professional (comes with Adobe Suite) as a downsized PDF and then uploaded to Kindle Create to make the fancy e-book. If the book is slow to load onto KDP, most likely the files are too fat (big). The book will have an increased cost on download due to the increase of the data. It is better to upload smaller file sizes because the savings is passed onto the author when it comes to the download of the book by the reader.*

Process used in our office to make a highly searchable book:

- Use KDP Rocket to find high-value search words for the book. https://publisherrocket.com/download/
- Make a summary using Ivorymind app. https://ivorymind.com/
- Put the summary and keywords into the properties menu within InDesign file as it is created. Then we make the paperback and hardbound book (if indicated) from these files.
- Make a separate e-book folder for the Kindle Create e-book. https://kdp.amazon.com/en_US/help/topic/GUGQ4WDZ92F733GC
- Delete page numbers (automatic pagination)
- Delete Table of Contents and Index
- Label all photographs using Object Export Options. In the newer InDesign program there are options for Custom and AI options. If I use the AI option, I always check for accuracy. The Structure option is for clip art, etc. If photographs are labeled in Photoshop properties they will flow over into InDesign.
- Can generate Alt Text in Word by clicking on the image and typing in the Alt Text for the image.
- Open Kindle Create App and enter the title of the book. Specify the type of book. I generally use Print Replica because it allows to make the hyperlinks all active while stabilizing the text and images.

**Note. Links that are long I bring into a software* https://tinyurl.com/ *to shorten them up. Links that are too long look unsightly in a book.*

Example--this is the link for purchase of my other marketing book:

https://www.amazon.com/Dynamic-Book-Marketing-Sheri-Hauser-ebook/dp/B0DBV7RPP5/ref=sr_1_2?crid=2AI260JL4VQBX&dib=eyJ2IjoiMSJ9.IV75qRedC3wXeWLcIXegh3MHDHWA_EFB0WHGt4358wkyE7Pr92bjVeuUC9n3mJAyDaWY6CfarjCV7vujxE2T0x9tS-Te4ET5uuZkxqdsAcZ9FVm18iXqCVj4vazaDe16zf0_h9x-

9ReYyE8K02RtgROuwME-o3qk3QReDRYnbgHAt0jtjSP0I2zvCHtX-2wQ9xYWeZaLWSaBXjvhDkxjmLz4vWjsjceVcpulhf1Lhzw2o.NqP50NlFHHj_z_F0WgoU0bg-n9xPhubuRZtRBgkgbh4&dib_tag=se&keywords=sheri+hauser&qid=1776968695&s=books&sprefix=sheri+haus%2Cstripbooks%2C329&sr=1-2

Here is the same link shortened:
https://tinyurl.com/2ahjucnu

Kindle Unlimited

KDP allows books to go into a program called *Kindle Unlimited.* https://www.amazon.com/kindle Amazon subscribers can register to read unlimited books per month on Kindle Unlimited, and Amazon pays authors based on the number of pages read. Many times, I have found readers will sample the book on Kindle Unlimited and then go on to purchase it.

Business cards similar to the one shown below are helpful to bring to events. The one below includes the QR Code, tiny url (in case someone doesn't have an ability to scan the code) and a place to write the date of the next date when the book will be offered for free.

Please return to Amazon and leave a book review.

Glorybound Publishing
sheri@gloryboundpublishing.com
Sheri Hauser

- Editing
- Publishing
- Marketing

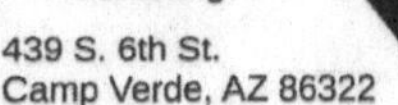

This part of 'equiping the saints' for the ministry; to enable them to freely share with others how to find and read their book.

We order the cards through Vistaprint https://www.vistaprint.com/

at a cost of $16 per 250. I have a professional account which offers 40% discount on everything I order with free mailing, so I can order the cards and have them sent directly to the author's address. I think of it as part of enabling them to be successful.

Kindle Unlimited https://www.amazon.com/kindle offers free ads several times per year for books registered in the program. Authors may select the time period, and the ad is displayed for 5 days. This is a good opportunity to provide notice to potential readers (who might also leave a book review).

I suggest that authors schedule and plan for the free-release dates. We have them develop an e-mail list of those they feel may be interested in purchasing their book (or reading it for free). I suggest around 50 emails. It is possible to send out a mass email to the recipients, but I do not feel this is the best. People rather hear from others personally, so I suggest setting up the email (copy and paste) while adding a personal note in the beginning.

You can set up a 5-day release and send out an email with the URL to purchase your book on Amazon. It will be free during this time, and readers can leave a verified book review. Just remember, they must have spent at least $50 within the last 12 months to leave a verified review.

Below is a sample of the email which I sent out when I released the marketing book a few weeks back. I sent out 49 emails and was able to boost the sale to 48 books for the first week—and this was the week before the free release.

Dear friend

New book--please give an unbiased review
Please help me out.
I am very excited to announce that the new book I have written **Dynamic Book Marketing 2026** has been released on Amazon! The e book is only $5.99. Download it today!
Please give it a read. I would really, really appreciate an unbiased honest review of the work which will help get the book going with sales.
Here is how to find the book. Please return to the bottom of the page and do the book review. Thank you so much!
It will be FREE for E Book April 13-17th
In order to help you out, here is a summary of my book.
Sheri Hauser, owner of Glorybound Publishing with over 20 years of experience and more than 800 books published, provides an extensive guide on modern book publishing, marketing, and sales strategies. She emphasizes the critical gap between writing a book and successfully marketing it. She provides expert advice into key insights, practical strategies, and industry knowledge. The comprehensive guide serves as a practical manual for authors navigating the complex landscape of modern book publishing, marketing, and sales, highlighting both proven strategies and common pitfalls.

To leave a review: Go to the page where the book is located and go down to the bottom of the page, on the left there is a button—Leave a Review—Then sign onto Amazon (if you have not already). When you sign on, it will direct you back to the page to leave a review. Add stars and then leave the review. Please give it a title of your review and post.
Click below to find my book on Amazon:
https://tinyurl.com/zypjvxv5
Here is a sample review to get you going:
Sample Review
Marketing is really key. The author emphasizes it is never too early to begin marketing. I am going to start right now…now that I know what to do. Thank you, Sheri Hauser for a book well written and useful for today.

Thank you very much!

Sheri Hauser

Author Central

Author Central provides a place where authors have a voice.
**from Google AI Search*
Benefits of Author Central:

- **Centralized book and bio page:** Create a single, dedicated page that lists all your books and includes your biography, photos, videos, blog feeds, and events.
- **Customizable URL:** Generate a unique, professional URL for your author page to make it easier for readers to find and share.
- **Monitor reviews:** View and respond to all book reviews in one place.
- **Add editorial reviews:** Showcase positive endorsements from professional reviewers to build credibility.
- **Improve search rankings:** A well-maintained Author Central page can improve your book's visibility in Amazon and Google search results.
- **Engage readers:** The "Follow" button allows customers to receive notifications about your new book releases.
- **Promote books:** Use Author Central's marketing tools, such as adding a "Search Inside" preview for eligible books, to increase discovery.
- **Promote events:** List book signings, readings, and other events to engage with your readership.
- **Cross-promote:** Link to your website, social media, and other online presences to keep readers engaged.

Author Website

Author Website
Many people believe that an author is not a professional author if he/she does not have a website. I am not entirely convinced this is true. I have been a webmaster working on websites for over 20 years. A website should have a purpose, otherwise it is money ill-spent.

Why do you feel you need a website?

How much will it cost?

Who will maintain it?

What profit will it bring you?

Working with the Chamber of Commerce for several years in my small town, I have seen a lot of websites; some fancy and others with broken links that look like somebody's 12-year-old nephew put them together.

Reasons to Have a Website

If you have several books for sale, it may be helpful, as the books are often not shown together elsewhere. It provides a place where shoppers can go, purchase one, and return to purchase the next book in the series.

Another reason for a website is if the author is an expert on an interesting subject. For instance, I recently released a local history book. This is the first compiled history book in the area, so other historians are curious as to other findings that may be uncovered. The website can be used to post old photos and letters that were not included in the published book. It provides a place for historians to meet with a common subject. When someone writes a book, it seems almost automatic that he/she becomes an *expert* in the field. Therefore, it makes sense for an expert to be one who runs an information gathering website.

If the book that was published is part of an outreach for an organization, then a website is essential. Of course, the book is not the primary focus, but rather adjunctive to the purpose of the organization. For example, my company put together a picture book for a philanthropic organization whose goal is to beautify the trails in a nearby town. They sponsored a mural along the walkway, and as it was painted, they shot photographs. The book was a compilation of the mural's construction and was given to the financial sponsors when the mural was completed. They needed a website to show their progress and gather financial donations. The book was posted on the website in addition to its original purpose.

Reasons Not to Have a Website

Some believe that when an author publishes a book, they have launched a business. In keeping with that reasoning, they assume that a business must have a website. As a general rule, publishing one book does not indicate you have a business—unless you are famous and everyone is waiting with open arms to purchase the book. Most new titles sell fewer than 100 copies in the first year. If the author has a low printing cost, he can glean a royalty of $5 or so. Five dollars x 100 books = $500 for the year. That is not commensurate with income from a business—it looks more like a hobby.

If you are setting up a website to prove the legitimacy of publishing a book, don't do it!

Also, if you have published only one or two books, then why not just tell people about the books on Facebook or via email? Unless you have a blog, there will be no reason for them to return to the website. People visit websites for information, to shop, and to connect with those of similar interests. If you only have a few items for them to shop for and do not present ongoing information, they will not return to the website.

Cost of the website

I have set up some pretty inexpensive websites because I am a webmaster skilled at putting them together. I can give people a good idea of how much a website will cost using GoDaddy and its templates, then building it yourself (or having your 12-year-old nephew do it). First you buy the domain name. It is like a street sign. The cost of domain names ranges from $2 to $2000 per year, depending on the value of the words. (Here we go again with the price of words. I purchased a domain name, *Miracules,* which is the title of my first book, several years ago for around $20. It is now worth over $2,000 because other people want it. They probably have products, etc., that feature the same word.)

Once you buy a domain name, you attach it to a property or a website. The two are separate until they are connected. Websites have all kinds of variables depending on the functionality desired. Simple websites cost around $120 per year. Websites with a shopping basket incur an additional $30 per month.

If you know what you are doing or are willing to dive in and learn what is needed, it is quite possible to use the templates on GoDaddy and make a nice-looking website for around $150 per year. If you have only one or two books to sell, it will most likely not pay for itself in sales.

If you do not know how to set up a website and hire a company or individual to do it for you, the prices vary widely. Shop around and make them show you functional websites they have built before you hire them to put yours together.

Website Maintenance

Generally, I update our websites every three months. I do not keep an active blog. Also, I disable live comments. When you set up a website, it will offer an option to make live questions/comments available to users while on the site. There is an additional charge to make it fully functional, an app to purchase, and you need to pay constant attention to answer when someone pops into the site with a question. Many website templates include the option to put in frequently asked questions, or FAQs. This is a good idea. Also, I add a contact page to encourage people to send emails for additional questions.

If you have a store, or are selling on the website, people can contact you via whatever email you have entered, and you can fulfill the purchase item by contacting the buyer.

Websites also offer a professional email address. If you have a website, this is a good option that does a few things:

It distances your personal email from the site, setting you away from scammers or pesky salesmen.

It helps to give a unified sales face. For example, my website is www.gloryboundpublishing.com My professional email for this site is sheri@gloryboundpublishing.com

I have email messages from the contact page (and sales) forwarded to my personal email, so I don't need to check two emails all the time.

My personal email would be cluttered with offers for SEO (which I receive nearly daily) if I used my personal email on the website.

We have several book marketing websites.

Book Marketplace

https://bookmarketplace.net	A Central Hub for lots of books
https://brainebook.com	Books to make you smart
https://awesomepoetry.shop	Poetry
https://womensbooks.shop	Women's books
https://Arizonabooks.shop	Arizona Books
https://historybooks.shop	History Books

Children's sites

https://animalbooks4kids.shop	Animal books for children
https://Bookstore4kids.com	Lots of books for children
https://homeschoolbooks.shop	Homeschool books for children
https://dogandcatbooks.shop	Dog and cat books for children

Christian Marketplace

https://godbookmarketplace.net	A central hub for Christian Marketplace
https://christianwomensbooks.shop	Christian Women's books
https://christianmensbooks.shop	Christian Men's Books

Authors may put up to 3 books by one author on 2 sites for $10/month. Go to one of the hubs to sign up for the book marketplace https://bookmarketplace.net or https://godbookmarketplace.net

Christian Book Marketing 2026

Section 1 General Book Marketing
Section 2 Selling Christian Books
Section 3 Target Marketing
- Finding the Ideal Client
- Develop A Spiel
- Find Your Audience
- Press Release
- E-mail Contacts
- Ready Made Audiences
- Book Festivals
- More Events

Section 4 Avenues of Marketing
Section 5 Recognizing a Marketing Scam
Section 6 Book Reviews
Section 7 Selling Used Books
Section 8 Book Awards
Section 9 Develop a Book Launch Plan

Section 3 →
Target Marketing

Finding the Ideal Client

Your Audience

All of us have an audience, which is a group of people we follow along with and interact with in one another's lives. The easiest place to start is with your audience. Where did Jesus send the disciples? They were to begin where they were and work from there. You will have the most success,just like the disciples, because these people already know and trust you. They probably have been hearing about the book for some time and are waiting for its release.

Figure Out Who is Your Ideal Client

When I graduated with the Social Media Marketing Diploma, one of the assignments was to identify my ideal client. To figure it out, you need to clearly identify what you are offering. Let's take a few examples so you can insert your service or product into the matrix.

What does Glorybound Publishing offer? Here is my spiel. (A "spiel" is a short, concise, prepared, often rehearsed, speech or monologue.)

Glorybound Publishing has been my company since 2005, publishing over 700 books. Presently, we are publishing four books per month. We focus on what I call difficult books. These are picture-intensive, full-bleed books, like history books and children's books, because we work with Adobe software, which includes InDesign and Photoshop. All of the books are put together in live sessions with the authors, and we charge by the hour, so authors have complete control over the expense and outcome of their books. We also have a sound room for making audiobooks. We can have authors Zoom in to record their own books or help with setting up their own equipment to record in their homes. Then they send us the audio files for edit and upload to ACX. And, finally, if someone already has a book but needs a little extra push with marketing, we have 11 topic-specific book marketing websites.

This incorporates several elements: It shows longevity of the business, indicating we have a proven track record, so we can be trusted with their book. Although we have worked on many books, we value each author as an individual, providing personalized, highly skilled services. We respect everyone's time and money, refusing to take advantage of anyone. We set ourselves apart, indicating that we handle projects other publishers cannot because of our education, skill, and experience as a business. Then I cap off the spiel with a final note—that if someone has already published their book, we can help to sell it by using our marketing websites. The spiel starts out impressive (with publishing over 700 books) and ends up impressive with a passing comment that we have 11 book marketing websites.

Now, let's go over a few titles, so you get the idea of how to incorporate your own into the process.

Yes Lord Yes Lord with a subtitle *Songs and music for children ages 0-12* by Marcy Lehman

Sample spiel: *Yes Lord Yes Lord is a book of 40 songs and music for children ages 0-12. I have been writing lyrics and songs for over 50 years and love sharing them with others. The book is perfect to share with Christian schools, churches, and camps. The songs are simple, and the music is uplifting, provided in piano lead sheets, chords, as well as ukulele. As a special bonus, I have released each song in video, which is perfect to follow along for beginners. Why continue to sing those tired, worn-out songs when there are fresh ones?*

This incorporates several elements: Marcy is experienced in music and lyrics. I go on to describe the book and then say who is the best customer for it. I focus on NEW songs and even give a little nudge at the end to instill guilt in those who continue to use worn-out material. People always migrate to something new, but you must build trust for them to switch from what they already know is proven. By telling them there are videos, they have an opportunity to 'test' the songs before using them with children.

First Day of School by Karna Peck. It is a children's book appropriate for age 4-7.

Sample spiel: *The book, First Day of School by Karna Peck, is perfect for ages 4-7 years old. It is colorfully illustrated with delightful characters and available in paperback, Kindle e-book, audiobook, and video. The story is not merely for entertainment, but to teach children to notice other children (at school) who are less fortunate and offer to share whatever is needed. In the story, a child (on his first day of school) has no one to help him get ready for school. A (child) angel sits next to him on the bus, sharing a snack, socks, and a comb. Karna Peck is a professional artist. Some time back, she worked as a homeless advocate, which touched her heart to reach out to children in need. The book raises awareness in the child (who is reading it) to look around and notice others in need,and help in simple ways. Who will teach the children to care? Why not begin with the first day of school?*

This incorporates several elements: I introduce the author with information that she is a professional artist with a heart for homeless children. The book is not for entertainment, but to teach a valuable lesson. I go into a few details about the book and give a challenge to purchase the book, which will help raise awareness for children to help one another.

Develop A Spiel

In your spiel, tell who you are, what you are doing and why others should listen to you. People are constantly bombarded with information. So, to get them to stop long enough to read yours, it needs to be catchy. What makes your book (or company) stand out from the rest? In all of the spiels above, I give enough information so that if the person reading the spiel does not need the item or service, he/she has what is required to share it further.

Authors need to take time to gather their project up, like folding the dishes into a tablecloth so that others can get a hold of it. If you weed out the fluff and the bright lights for someone, it really helps to provide an opportunity so they can make their own decision about whether this is worthwhile or not. Many sales promotions "cram it down their throats" and are quickly refused.

So, who is your ideal client? Who is the best one to purchase your book?

Glorybound Publishing's ideal client is a 78-year-old guy with two houses and a flip phone.
What that means is he is well retired and probably has something to say (a manuscript in the drawer). Having two houses proves he has expendable income (enough to be able to afford to publish a book). But he is digitally challenged—being raised in a nondigital world.

The ideal client for the Yes Lord Yes Lord song book is a 36-year-old music teacher at a Christian elementary school.
What that means is she is young enough to want new songs, has students who can use them, and wants a Christian music slant.

The ideal client for First Day of School is a 40-year-old male kindergarten teacher.
What this means is that he cares about young children, is within the environment, and understands the needs of those who do not have someone to help them get ready for school. He is tired of books that simply 'entertain,' and is looking to feed young minds with moral fiber. I think this book can also be used in homeschool programs.

Find Your Audience

First, you need to figure out what you have, why it is valuable, and figure out who else would consider what you have useful as well. The next step is to map out a route to bring the information to the ideal client. Where is he or she?

The first sample (my business) is looking for an older guy with money and a manuscript, but he is not on social media. It would do no good to run a media blitz on Facebook because many of these types are not on Facebook. If, perhaps, I had a cookbook with an ideal client profile being a 70-year-old woman, I could find her on Facebook. Elderly women generally keep up with the grandchildren using Facebook, but men, not so much. So, where can I go to find such a guy?

I joined Alignable (a small business social media site) a few years back. What I found is there are many people who have already retired and are tinkering at home-based businesses. They are done with the general workforce. Alignable is a fairly easy digital network which offers several interactive meetings, the goals of which are to link with other businesses. You sign up for a meeting and during the hour they put you in 6-minute breakout rooms with another person. The breakout connections are based on the keywords (this should start sounding familiar) you put in on your profile indicating who your ideal client is. I said that I am looking for authors. Consequently, each time I sign up for an Alignable connection meeting, the matrix pairs me with authors. Perfect.

This is crazy, but nearly every time I go to one of those meetings, I obtain a new client! What I have found is that many have a nonpublished book in the drawer and if they found someone they could trust, they would be happy to publish the book. It seems to me they have entered into their profile somewhere that they are authors, otherwise they would not be connected with me in a session. Publishing is difficult today because most is done online, working on a screen, and with people you are not sure are located in the United States or not. (Again, notice that I have honed in on their insecurity with the internet. They want to work with someone they can see. I promise to do the books in live sessions, so they immediately jump onto the deal.)

Yes Lord Yes Lord audience. Finding a Christian School Music teacher is easy. Contact the schools in your area—or beyond. This book can also go to churches and Christian camps. I think mailing a flyer or offering a deal when the book is free can be helpful.

The First Day of School audience is at a school, a homeschool situation or a homeless center. All of these places would be interested in the book. Because Karna is a professional artist, perhaps some budding artists may be interested in using it as a reference to create their own pictures. She is an art teacher, so she can encourage her students to purchase the book.

Now…insert your own title, figure out what the message of it is, and who is your ideal client.

Press Release

A press release is one page of information which includes:

Author biography with something unique about him/her

Summary of the book

Book cover and price

Where it can be purchased from (local or online)

May include a QR Code

The press release can be changed up along the way according to events and distribution points. The idea is to work with a local distribution option, make sure they have some books, and send potential buyers to them. They benefit, and you obtain sales.

Dynamic Book Marketing 2026

Key Points of the Dynamic Book Marketing 2026 Book

Marketing must begin early, ideally during manuscript development. Author's goal clarity drives marketing strategy effectiveness. Multiple book formats (print, e-book, audio-book) maximize exposure. Amazon algorithms favor sales velocity, verified reviews, and paid ads.

Keyword research and metadata optimization are vital. Networking and using ready-made audiences lower marketing costs. Professional presentation (cover design, press releases, spiels) is essential.

Local bookstore placement requires relationship-building and professionalism. Avoid marketing scams by researching and verifying companies. Building genuine reviews consistently over time is crucial. Participation in book awards can enhance reputation but requires investment.

Author websites are optional and should have a clear purpose and maintenance plan. This comprehensive guide by Sheri Hauser serves as a practical manual for authors navigating the complex landscape of modern book publishing, marketing, and sales, highlighting both proven strategies and common pitfalls.

Dynamic Book Marketing 2026 by Sheri Hauser
Published by Glorybound Publishing
ISBN 978-1-60789-676-0
Paperback, E-Book, Audio-book on Amazon

Publisher and Author—Sheri Hauser

Sheri Hauser, owner of Glorybound Publishing with over 20 years of experience and more than 800 books published, provides an extensive guide on modern book publishing, marketing, and sales strategies. She emphasizes the critical gap between writing a book and successfully marketing it. This summary distills her expert advice into key insights, practical strategies, and industry knowledge.

- **Sheri Hauser** founded Glorybound Publishing in 2005.
- Published over 800 books, some with extensive photos and complex layouts.
- Expertise includes Adobe InDesign, Photoshop, audiobook production, and social media marketing with diplomas in Sound Engineering and Social Media Marketing.
- Recognized as Small Business of the Year twice and ranked in the Top 50 Businesses on Alignable 2025.
- Active community involvement and award-winning creativity.

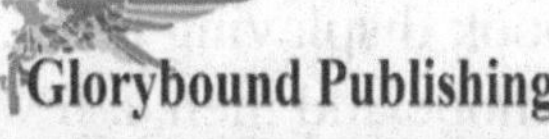

Contact Sheri Hauser at:
sheri@gloryboundpublishing.com

www.gloryboundpublishing.com

E-mail Contacts

The email contact list is a perfect place to distribute a press release, along with promoting upcoming events you will be part of in the near future. E-mail contact lists are a virtual treasure trove of contacts who will be happy to hear of your successful publishing of a book. It takes a while, but you can set up a group and send out a mass e-mail if you want. It is easier to set up groups on g-mail than Yahoo (I feel). I have done this and found that once a month (for updates) is more than enough. If you send out too many, people will become overwhelmed and unsubscribe or block you. See Section 2 for sample.

Ready-Made Audiences

The least expensive traction for book author's exposure is to use other people's audiences. This does not mean to use people! What it means is that if there is a fair, set up a table with your book. Whoever is advertising the fair is making an audience for all of the vendors at the place to sell and show their wares. You are not surprising them by using their ready-made audience!

Facebook

Facebook is a good place to start. Remember that Facebook only shows a limited number of posts from those you are in contact with, so you may need to do a bit of dancing to figure out how to reach a broader audience. There is a matrix with Facebook displaying posts, etc. Have you shopped for something on your phone and then, a few hours later, when you are on Facebook, you see an advertisement for something similar? They are gathering data from your search and using it for marketing purposes.

If you are going to use Facebook, then spend some time learning how the matrix works. I do not want to go into it here—but suffice to say, "Post often and comment on others'posts." This will expand your reach.

Join Facebook groups. There are several Christian writers' groups. They have tips and people there support one another. Don't be afraid to support someone who is struggling with their writing. That is what Christians do.

Make the cover of your book 'live' and post it on Facebook often. There is no limit to the number of times you can post something. But… mix it up so people won't feel spammed. To make the cover of your book 'live,' go to Amazon, where it is sold. Open the version of the book you wish to advertise on Facebook. Copy all of the information in the top URL line of the page. This is the 'address' of your book on Amazon. I suggest putting the URL address on a page where you can retrieve it as needed. Now, go to Facebook and begin to make a post. You might say something like, "Here is my new book. It was just released on Amazon. Check it out." Then take the URL address (it will be long) and paste it into the post. What will happen is the address will become hidden, and a picture of the front of your book will materialize. Voila!

The Kindle e-book will be available on Amazon.
Free Book date ______

To download the free book,
https://tinyurl.com/zypjvxv5

When you set up a free 5-day book release on *Kindle Unlimited,* then tell your Facebook friends they can read the book. Remember, you can beg for reviews, but you cannot trade or give anything of value to obtain them. So, if you tell folks that you are offering your book for free, you can return the next day or so and remind them that reader reviews really help authors to gain traction on Amazon. It is possible to send chat messages to individuals if you are sure they don't want to miss out on the free book reading.

Some people set up Author Facebook Pages. If you want to gather supporters and have something to say (on an ongoing basis), then this is a good idea. It can replace a website in many ways.

Spin-off Books from Successful Ventures

Many professionals grow in their careers and write a "How To" book. It is easy to sell the book to anyone entering the business wanting to copy their success. Examples are chefs (who own a restaurant), financial planning experts (with advice and tips) and pastors of large congregations (how I did it). I put together a checklist for those renting Air BNB properties, compiled by a Realtor who runs several Air BNBs in the local area. She has a ready market for sales of her books. My sister teaches art at a local community college. She has a couple of art instruction books. Do you think she sells them to her students? Sure, she does. They purchase her book for the same reason they purchase the chef's book—to copy her success.

All of these are representative of Ready-Made Audiences because the author already has an audience. He just needs to tell his audience there is a book!

*Note: There is an ongoing situation with Christian leaders (who have a ready-made audience) paying someone to write a book, put their name on it, and making a personal profit from the sales. Pastors with large congregations appear to coerce (or guilt) congregants into purchasing their book. It seems to be an ethical situation. Is it OK for him or her to profit from the church? Does he or she use their position to pressure sales?

There is a difference between the situation as I stated above and someone (even a pastor) writing a book and putting it out there to share. There is a fine line because, if the pastor honestly believes someone's life will be better by reading his book, then he may pressure that person to buy the book. Does the pastor make money from the sales? Yes.

Some see this as a trap of the enemy and make provisions to not keep the money for themselves, but return it back to the congregation. I don't know the answer—you will have to work it out with God. But, I know it is a problem.

As a Christian writer, you may find yourself in a position of leadership. How you handle this ethical question is personal.

Groups You Already Belong To

Groups that you already belong to are perfect opportunities for the presentation of your book. Keep in mind you are presenting the book, not selling it. Think of it like your daughter doing a ballet recital. Everyone goes there and is focused on the dancers. They pay to get into the show, but don't buy the dancers. There is exposure of the dancing group. It is not like a dance for money, and the girls do not earn anything from it. The book is like the daughter on stage. You present it (her) to them. Ask if they want to see it. If you make the book free every so often, then even those without money will be able to get into the show! Remember, those who get a book during the free-book time on Amazon KDP can leave a review. The review may be totally worth the effort of contacting them and providing a free book.

Many authors keep a book in their car…and as they go through the day and people (who are in the groups they belong to) ask about it, they show it to them. It is show and tell!

Who You Know

I opened a sound studio a few years back. It did not take long for me to realize I needed more education on how to make audiobooks. So, I went to an online school and obtained a Sound Engineering diploma. After that, the school asked me if I wanted to study something else. I knew they were just trying to make money, but I figured, "Why not?"

So, I decided to pursue a diploma in Social Media Marketing. After graduating from the program, I joined a small business social media organization called *Alignable*. I set up a home page and began making connections. Quickly, I gained recognition as Business Person of the Year in my town. Continuing to gather connections, Alignable (with their matrix) started seeing me as a valuable connector—or a main hub connector. The following year, I once again garnered the title of Business Person of the Year. The following year, I decided to increase my goals and reached out to more connections than ever. I reached over 3000 connections, and when the contest for Business Person of the Year occurred, I obtained the honor of being one of the top 50 Business

Persons of the United States and Canada (on all of Alignable), with over 9 million businesses. I finished at number 25. I figured I needed to keep pushing until the last moment, so I wouldn't get pushed off the list!

One of the core principles of Alignable is, "It's not who you know, but who your connections might know." What that means is that the person you may be communicating with may not need your service or product, but if your presentation is tight and the service or product seems valuable, others will refer you to their friends or acquaintances. Presently, I have nearly 4K connections and gain on average 4 new clients (authors) per month. I have over 550 positive reviews. Potential clients read my page, which tells what the business offers, see the positive reviews, and talk to folks whose books I have published. What happens is that those coming to me are not *potential clients*, but already know they want my services. This is the power of referral. So, as you talk about your book where ever you are, just talk. Don't worry if the person you are talking to seems like a potential buyer, because maybe he or she knows someone who will benefit from the book and will refer that person to you.

Book Festivals

Book Festivals are generally organized by a book club or the local library. They charge a low fee to authors, inviting them to set up a table and show their books. The festival will ask for authors to submit their biography, a photo, and some information related to the books that they will be offering at the event so they can do PR and make brochures ahead of time. Sometimes they have educational talks. It is best to have a goal of showing your book, rather than selling the book, because as a general rule, most authors only sell a few books.

Planning for a book festival: There is a transition from writing college papers to writing a professional book, and it should be evident in what you present. Part of becoming professional is setting up a mojo . Tables are usually 8-10 feet long. It is a good idea to bring a tablecloth (I buy lightweight waterproof fabric shower curtains that are the same color as my logo). If the event is outdoors, I provide a way to tack down the tablecloth. At the very minimum, you should bring business cards that tell others who you are, the name of the book, and how to order it. I recommend a simple banner (like those available from Vistaprint) featuring the book cover that can be displayed along the back wall or on the front of the table. Pull-out or pop-up banners are popular as well. Book board signs are more difficult to display but can be read across the room. I bring no more than 20 books to the event. If it is outside, or there is some distance between the parking lot and where the event will be held, I recommend putting the books into a rolling ice chest. You can put other items on top of the ice chest and move it along easily. If the weather turns foul during an outside event, you can store the books in the ice chest, where they will be protected from the elements. It is nice to display a few books on a stand on the table; inexpensive ones can be found at Ross or Hobby Lobby. Some authors get creative and make their own book stands.

When you have a lot of books—or a series of books—you may want to invest in an expandable bookshelf appropriate to the size of your books. I have one and keep it in its box, pulling it out whenever we need it. To plan for the event, I set it up in my office and have my office manager fill it with books. Then she removes the books and packs them separately for the trip to the event. This way, we can set up quickly, because everything is preplanned.

Some events require a pop-up tent. I purchased one online that matches my logo color. Event spaces are always rented as 10'x10' spaces, so an average tent will work well. I suggest buying the sturdiest one you can afford. The low-cost tents will fail when you need them most—in inclement weather.

Our pack-and-go book event kit includes:

- Tent (if it is outside)
- 2 fold-out tables (6' x 2')
- Two table covers
- Book stands (2 for larger books and 4 for smaller size books)
- Mascot (We have a big stuffed frog as the mascot for our children's books and he looks nice sitting on the table next to the books. He is indestructible and he doesn't mind being smashed into a container).
- A plastic container of books with a lid. Again, if it is outside, and may be stormy, we prepare for it.
- We have a large vinyl advertising banner that has Velcro along the top and loops along the bottom. We can attach it to the side of the tent for protection from the sun, wind or rain. It is a sturdy sign with large lettering that can be seen across the event.
- We bring a couple of flags. Some events do not permit certain types of flags, so I advise you check on this prior to packing them. We have our logo on a 1ft x 1.5 ft flag, and we were creative, attaching it to a pull-out painting handle. We affixed a rod to keep the flag extended. We can bungee the flagpole and extend the pull-out to several feet above the tent, helping shoppers locate our booth. I have ordered several of these types of small flags for authors with their book on each flag. They fly it above their area. You can insert the flagpole into an umbrella stand as well if the event is inside.

We also make sure we have the ability to take money. Many people do not carry cash these days, and you will sell more books if you offer the option to pay by credit card, Zelle (https://www.zelle.com/), Venmo (https://venmo.com/), or PayPal (https://www.paypal.com/).

The most common small business credit card app is Square Up. You attach a bank account where you want the money to go, and they send a penny to the account. You confirm it, and the account becomes active. It takes about a week to get it going because of all the confirmations. It is not necessary for you to be a licensed business to set up such an account; any individual can set one up. I advise putting your name as the 'business' on the receipt and omitting your personal address. It is free to set up and charges a small fee for each purchase. (https://app.squareup.com/login)

Usually, with book events, they will request each table to submit a book. Then later in the day, they have a drawing with an opportunity to win free books. Sometimes they use them as raffle items. At the start of the event, I generally locate the sponsor and hand over my submission. The sooner the better, because they will display all of the submissions on a prize table—you may as well take advantage of their PR.

Most commonly, I see authors rush in to set up, bring 50 books, have homemade business cards, and neglect to talk to other vendors. They see the other vendors as competitors rather than working together to sell everyone's book. They sit stone-faced, waiting for someone to come along and buy their book. When books don't sell as briskly as they hoped, they become sad. Talk to other vendors. They are potential customers.

The best way to enjoy a book fair is to prepare in advance by setting up everything at your house. Fix the table the exact way you want it to look while at the event. Put all of the items on the table (including books) and evaluate how it looks. Make changes… and pack only the items you need. Make an effort to minimize the setup and have a 'face' for the table. The colors, brochures, bookmarks, business cards, press releases, banners, and flags should match. That is called "Branding." If you are not familiar with the term, do a bit of research. Your book becomes the pivotal point for your brand (unless you have a series—and then you should have a logo which will help others to connect the group). *Tip: If you order from Vistaprint, they make suggestions regarding branding. (https://www.vistaprint.com/)

More Events

Local Events that invite people to set up a table. Some require a business license, but most are inexpensive and do not. Just check when registering. **Women of the Moose** was one of my best festivals! Don't reject an invitation to attend an event because it was not a book event. Again, consider your target audience. Will some of those people be at the event?

Do not allow the cost to deter you from attending an event. If you are challenged to come up with the fees to be in an event, often, if you volunteer to help out with it, they will give you a courtesy booth spot. Free is good.

As a rule, if I am invited to an event, I give it a try. If it is not a good fit for me to attend, I forego it next time. For example, we were invited to a festival at the local Christian school. We quickly discovered that sticky little fingers are not a good place to put our nice children's books on display. This was before I understood the value of recognizing the ideal client. We brought children's books to a children's event. The books are not sold to children, but adults. We turned our staff into book babysitters!

Don't Forget the Educational Sector

OLLI (Osher Lifelong Learning Institute)

* Osher Lifelong Learning Institutes offer noncredit courses with no assignments or grades to adults over age 50. Since 2001, philanthropist Bernard Osher has made grants from the Bernard Osher Foundation to launch OLLI programs at 120 universities and colleges throughout the United States. (https://www.osherfoundation.org/olli.html)

OLLI has a couple of campuses nearby, so I registered as an instructor and taught some classes on publishing. There are no prerequisites to become an instructor—you just have to be willing to teach something for free. The organization uses classrooms at various colleges and charges a small fee for those wanting to attend the classes. There is everything from Current Events Lunch and Learn, to The Space Program, to Dancing with Amy…you get the idea. The classes are a few weeks at a time. I signed up to teach a class, "How to Be a Children's Book Artist." The school handles all of the advertising and registration, and sets up the classrooms. I showed up and taught my lesson to 24 adult students, for two sessions per week for five weeks. From the class, several students followed me to become published through my company. It provided a great way to help the community as well as gain authors.

Oftentimes, when an author writes a book, he or she is noted as an expert in the field. If you write a history book, then this is what you can teach. If you write a children's book, you can teach *sharing lessons to children*. The advantage of being an OLLI Instructor is that the students come to you—you are not coming to them. They want to hear what you have to say. With the OLLI around here, the authors are not supposed to sell books during class, but they bring them in their car and students purchase them in the parking lot.

Christian Book Marketing 2026

Section 1 General Book Marketing
Section 2 Selling Christian Books
Section 3 Target Marketing
Section 4 Avenues of Marketing
- Wholesale Books
- Retail Books Directly to Customers
- Print with Direct Distribution
- Seller Central
- Selling Books Directly to Local Bookstores
- A Basic Plan to See Books In Bookstores

Section 5 Recognizing a Marketing Scam
Section 6 Book Reviews
Section 7 Selling Used Books
Section 8 Book Awards
Section 9 Develop a Book Launch Plan

Section 4 →
Avenues of Marketing (Wholesale, etc)

Wholesale Books

The primary distributor of wholesale books is IngramsSpark. The biggest benefit of IngramsSpark is that your book enters Ingram's distribution list, which automatically makes it available to any brick-and-mortar bookstore in the US. Also, it automatically appears on bookshop.org, every indie bookstore's online stores, and anywhere else that uses Ingram's automatic data feed for their bookstores. IngramsSpark is crucial for reaching bookstores and libraries due to its vast distribution network, though it has a more complicated user interface and requires setting a wholesale discount.

There are no fees to upload the book and list it for sale. Additional fees are assessed to make changes to files after a certain period of time.

IngramsSpark offers the books at 55% less than the listed retail price. They pass 40% on to retailers and keep 15%.

Royalty to the author equals the book's retail price, minus the print price, minus 55%. The sales surcharge is 1% of the book's list price and will be deducted from the compensation earnings each time the book is sold. The royalty is substantially less than when using KDP.

Retailers purchase the books from IngramsSpark at the wholesale price. Authors are not informed who purchased the books. The retailer may return the unsold books to IngramsSpark for a refund. The author is billed for the refunded books and has an option to have them sent to him/her or destroyed.

Taken from: https://www.reddit.com/r/selfpublish/comments/uck6pf/ingramspark_cost/

Retail Books Directly to Customers

Amazon KDP (Kindle Direct Publishing)

In 2018, CreateSpace was purchased by KDP [Kindle Direct Publishing], and it is a wonderful way for self-published authors to release their books directly to the general market. The print prices are low, and the books are print-on-demand. Authors keep a significant percentage of royalties from the sales.

There are several advantages to putting book files directly onto KDP. Let me emphasize that you are putting your book FILES onto KDP, not your book. If you have a book that is already printed and bound, then you should release it on Seller Central. They have a couple of programs. You can either send copies which are stored in a warehouse until they are sold, or hang onto the copies, and if someone orders one, Amazon will inform you and you can mail out the copy.

KDP is designed to be like getting a candy bar from a vending machine. You insert a quarter, and the machine spits out a Snickers bar. With KDP, you upload the files and, when individuals order the book, KDP, in conjunction with Amazon, fills the order, prints, binds, and mails out the book to the customer. Then they pay the author a royalty. Just like that!

If I upload a paperback book, generally that title is 'live' within 24 hours. What that means is people from all over the globe (or in areas you specify) can order it; Amazon will print, bind, and mail it out right away. E-books are released immediately after the book is uploaded. As soon as the books become 'live,' I can produce an ad and begin selling the book. It is a clear advantage.

Low Print Price

KDP offers a low print price. Generally, the print price is half what we would pay for a conventional printer. Recently, I had an author print his book (90 pages 8.5" x 11" full color with 200 pictures). It cost him $14 each to print. When I began working with KDP, I suggested putting his book on on that platform. We put it on KDP and his print price—for exactly the same book—was $7.00. Immediately, he called me and asked me to drop the selling price of his book. The lower print price permitted him to offer a lower retail price. On average, books cost us between $2.50 and $3.75 to print through the KDP options. With a retail price of between $10.50 and $16.95, authors rake in a royalty payment of between $4.60 and $7.20.

It is clear to me, after working with books for 20 years, that Amazon favors those who use KDP. They trust the authors are writing their own books and selling their own books (unlike Seller Central—where you can sell anyone's book). Libraries use Seller Central to offload used books.

As soon as you upload a book to Amazon, it hits the international market (providing you set it up that way). I put a book up for an author last week, and within 24 hours, she sold 143 books in 9 countries! This was enabled because we released the book in both paperback and e-book formats. E-books are very popular among those who do not want to wait for a book to be mailed. They are also cost-effective because they do not involve paper and distribution.

KDP allows you to upload the information about a book and then come back around the corner and upload the body and the cover (fillet version). A few of the preliminary elements (such as title and author) are not changeable after you approve the uploaded files. However, you can quite easily upload new inner files and a new cover if you want to change it.

One of the problems that independent authors encounter is they need an ISBN for their book. Bowker's Link sells ISBN numbers. I know because I own 1000 of them. Generally, they cost around $10 each. However, Bowker's only sells them to publishers. Independent authors have a difficult time obtaining an ISBN for their book title, which is essential for cataloging by libraries and for it to be sold on conventional markets. Up to this time, authors had to 'invent' a publishing company just to get numbers from Bowker's Link for their books. Recognizing this problem, KDP opted to supply a free ISBN to anyone who wishes to publish their paperback using KDP. I think CreateSpace did this as well—because I have some authors left over from CreateSpace with ISBN numbers from them. Anyway, if you attempt to put a book on KDP, it requires you to have an ISBN.

You can use one of your own (as I have done for all of the books which I already printed and which are copyrighted by the US Copyright Office) or you can use theirs. I have put both into several books and they don't seem to mind. It is a good benefit for authors, and you are assured the numbers are valid because they come straight from KDP. E-Books do not need an ISBN when they are uploaded to KDP, but I recommend adding one if you have one available. This is because it helps to differentiate the book from others that may have similar or the same titles.

Print with Direct Distribution

Many choose to publish, print, and release their own titles with direct distribution from their office, church, school, or website. Manuals, Bible study booklets and children's learning materials are some examples of this type of print with direct distribution. The Glorybound Lasertrain has over 400 templates for compiling various types of books. The patterns are given in their respective software, and the print sets explain in detail how to use full-size and desktop printers to produce a specific item. See the Glorybound Lasertrain. https://thepublisherschool.com/lasertrain

Seller Central

Books that are printed conventionally may be offered on Amazon through a program called Seller Central. It is simple to open an account and submit photos of the book. They accept new and used editions. This is a good option for someone with a stack of books in their garage. Many libraries offload used books on Seller Central, making money on valuable titles. (See Section 6 for Apps that figure out how much a used book is worth.)

To sell books through Seller Central on Amazon, first create a seller account, then list books by finding them in the Amazon catalog using the ISBN, title, or by scanning the barcode with the Seller App. After finding the book, click "sell this product," select the condition, set a price, and choose the fulfillment method to complete the listing.

Fulfillment By Amazon (FBA) means the physical book is sent to Seller Central and stored in a warehouse. When someone orders the title, they mail it out to the individual. Fulfillment By Merchant (FBM) means that the merchant (the one who is storing the book) sends it to those who order it. The cost for Seller Central is $1 per item or unlimited for $40 (in 20250. If the seller opts to use FBA, then the book must be mailed to Seller Central, which will charge a storage fee.

This is how used books are posted on Amazon. It is popular with college students seeking used textbooks, as well as rare book dealers.

Selling Books Directly to Local Bookstores

To introduce yourself to a bookstore, research the store to see if your book is a good fit, and then prepare a concise pitch that highlights the book's appeal to their customers. Call ahead to identify the right person to speak with, and in your brief introduction, be polite, explain your connection (e.g., local author), and present why the book would be a good addition to their shelves.

Before You Go

Research the store: Visit the bookstore or check their website to understand its specific audience, genres, and community focus. This will help you tailor your pitch.

Identify the book buyer: Call the store to find out who the book buyer or manager is and what their preferred method of contact is (e.g., appointment, drop-in).

Prepare your materials: Have a professional-looking sell sheet or flyer, and bring a copy of your book—ideally a final copy or an Advance Reader Copy (ARC). Make sure the book has a professionally designed cover and that the title and the author's name are on the spine.

During your introduction

Be polite and concise: Acknowledge their busy schedule and keep your introduction brief. For example, you can say, "I know you're busy, but I'm a local author, and I love your bookstore. I'd only take a moment of your time."

Introduce your book: Briefly describe your book and what makes it unique, focusing on what would appeal to their specific customers.

Explain why it fits: Connect your book to their store's identity. For example, you could say, "My book is a good fit because I know you have a strong history section, and mine is about local history."

Discuss terms: Be prepared to discuss sales terms, such as consignment, which lowers the risk for the bookstore.

Offer support for an event: Ask if they would host an author signing or reading, and be ready to explain your marketing plan to promote the event and drive customers to the store.

After the introduction

Follow up professionally: Thank them for their time and provide your contact information.

Be persistent and patient: Booksellers are busy, so it's important to be persistent and follow up politely if you don't hear back immediately.

Ai

Best Practices For Authors Who Want Their Book In Bookstores

One of the most thrilling experiences an author can have is walking into a bookstore and finding their book on the shelves. I've seen authors giddy in these moments when they find their book stacked alongside a title by an author they've long admired, when they walk into a local Barnes & Noble and track down their own book. But this experience of moseying into your local bookstore and finding that they have your book stocked is the exception, not the norm. Small bookstores, especially, simply don't have the space to accommodate the many thousands of books being published each year.

For self-published authors, getting into bookstores is a chore. And it's not a given for traditionally published (and many hybrid-published) authors who have traditional distribution. Authors tend to get limited information from their publishers, often because their publishers have access to limited information from their distributors. For instance, authors I work with often ask me, "Which bookstores are carrying my book?" As a publisher, I can see which stores have ordered directly from our distributor, but I can't tell which stores might have ordered from third-party wholesalers, like Baker & Taylor and Ingram Wholesale. The reason authors pose this question is because they want to do follow-up with those bookstores. Still, I posit that the better approach is proactive, and rather than sending buyers to bookstores you know are carrying your book, you want to send them to the bookstore that's most convenient to them.

A Basic Plan to see Books in Bookstores

- Go introduce yourself to the book buyers at your local bookstores before your publication date. If you live in a small town, you may have zero or one bookstore, while bigger metropolitan areas may have many more. Where I live, for instance, there are ten bookstores, and many more in the broader area. You might want to narrow your efforts if you're lucky enough to live in an area with so many bookstores.

- Bring a copy of your ARC (Advance Reader Copy) when you go, and if you have a press release or a one-sheet (a flyer that highlights information about your book and includes endorsements), stick it inside. If you're not printing ARCs, wait to introduce yourself until you have a final copy of your book that you can bring in with you.

- It's unlikely that a book buyer will take an appointment with you if you call on the phone, so your best bet is to call ahead of time, ask who that person is, and find out when they'll be in the store. When you approach them, be uber-polite and respectful of their time. Here are some sample talking points:

- *"I know how busy you are, and I will only take 30 seconds of your time. I'm a local author, and I love your bookstore. My book is coming out next month, and I intend to drive customers into the store. I was hoping to leave this copy of my ARC [or book] with you so you'll remember me when people come in asking for it."*

- If you're a traditionally or hybrid published author, let them know who your publisher and/or distributor is. If you're self-published, say your book is available through Ingram (and make sure it is available through Ingram). Do not mention the "A-word." Bookstores do not want to hear about Amazon and they especially don't want to hear that your book is available through CreateSpace.

-

- Don't make mention of Amazon on your one-sheet either. Thank them for their time and be prepared to walk away. If the book buyer doesn't have follow-up questions for you, you're done. Do not hold them hostage or insist that they order your book or beg for an event. Your only job here is to make a first impression.

- Once your book is published, send people to the bookstore! This is one of the biggest conundrums I see in book publishing. Authors want their books in bookstores, but they're sending buyers to Amazon rather than to their local bookstores. We are so trained by our instant-access culture to get what we want right away that authors want consumers to have their book immediately upon publication. Amazon has also trained us to send buyers their way. Authors get spikes in their rankings on Amazon when they drive traffic to their listings. Amazon is increasingly trying to squeeze out any reviews of books not purchased on Amazon. And yet (obvious as this is, it's not widely practiced), if you want your book to be available in bookstores, you need to be sending people to bookstores.

- Whether you're making the ask in person or via a newsletter, explain to your prospective buyer the value (to you) of them going to their local bookstore and asking for the book. The bookstore will order the book if they don't have it on hand. It might take a couple of days, but they can and will get it for your customer. Many bookstores also ship. You might explain to said prospective buyer why it's important to support indie bookstores in this way, even when they have the free shipping that comes with Amazon Prime.

- Include a button on your website that encourages readers to go to a particular store. If it's a big enough independent bookstore, like Book Passage in Marin County, California; Elliott Bay in Seattle; or Tattered Cover in Denver, you can link the button directly to your book's buy page. This is a great way to cultivate good relationships with indies.

- Although this is a final note, it's an important one for self-published authors specifically. Before you do ANY of these things, make sure your book will pass muster with a book buyer. The Independent Book Publishers Association has published an Industry Standards Checklist for a Professionally Published Book. If you want bookstores to carry your book, please make sure you can check every single box on this list before you bring a copy into their store and ask them to carry it.
- Carry on, authors. Good luck, and please share with me and other readers any insights or lessons learned from your own experience.

https://www.huffpost.com/entry/best-practices-for-authors-who-want-their-book-in-bookstores_b_596e0e68e4b05561da5a5a97

Christian Book Marketing 2026

Section 1 General Book Marketing
Section 2 Selling Christian Books
Section 3 Target Marketing
Section 4 Avenues of Marketing
Section 5 Recognizing a Marketing Scam
Clues to Recognize a Marketing Scam
Section 6 Book Reviews
Section 7 Selling Used Books
Section 8 Book Awards
Section 9 Develop a Book Launch Plan

Section 5 →

Recognizing a Marketing Scam

Clues to recognize a marketing scam

- Many scammers call your personal cell phone. (How did they get that number?)
- They know a lot of information about your book and recite portions of it, indicating how impressed they are with it. (All of this information can be gathered through AI and SnapChat.)
- They focus on the VALUE of the book, indicating it has been neglected, and they want to ensure others see the VALUE of it. (A book is like a baby to an author—and they know this, so they play upon the value of the book to the author.)
- They seem to be intuitive, knowing that sales are down. (Sales information on all books is easily obtained through several software options: KDP Rocket or AuthorCentral.)
- They offer to do it for free because they see the value in the book and KNOW it will do well on the market if it is given a chance. (They put off asking for money right away, knowing they will be automatically rejected if they request money up-front.)
- They ALWAYS cost money. (They trade empty promises for cash—or a credit card number.)
- Do they put a time limit on the deal that they are offering?

- Many offer to re-publish the book because they see the potential of sales and know it can be so much better? (Of course, the author will be billed for their service.)

- Check on the company to see if it is legitimate.

- Put the company name into the search engine and ask who else has had problems with them. A search will often reveal their value.

- Is it in the US? Where is it based?

- Do they have a phone number listed on their website?

- Are they always calling you, but don't give you a number to call them back?

- Ask reputable authors and writers' groups if they know this company.

Christian Book Marketing 2026

Section 1 General Book Marketing
Section 2 Selling Christian Books
Section 3 Target Marketing
Section 4 Avenues of Marketing
Section 5 Recognizing a Marketing Scam
Section 6 Book Reviews
- Amazon Customer Reviews
- Prohibited Content and Actions
- Permitted Content and Actions
- Giving Books Away to Get Reviews
- Verified Reviews
- Posting Verified Reviews to Amazon
- Getting More Book Reviews
- Videos

Section 7 Selling Used Books
Section 8 Book Awards
Section 9 Develop a Book Launch Plan

Section 6 →
Book Reviews

Amazon Customer Reviews

*To submit a review, customers can find the book in **Your Orders** or go to the reviews section of the book page and select **Write a product review**. After they submit a review, the Amazon Community team will check if it meets the Community Guidelines.

Amazon book review guidelines prohibit reviews with financial or personal connections to the author and reviews that are manipulated through compensation, such as cash, discounts, or free products. Reviews must be the reviewer's honest opinion, cannot contain insults or misinformation, and should follow the general community guidelines for content. While authors can provide free or discounted copies, they cannot require a review in exchange or try to influence it.

Prohibited Content and Actions

- No compensation: Do not write a review for cash, discounts, free products, gift cards, or a refund.
- No close connections: Avoid reviews from friends, family, or business associates of the author.
- No review swapping: Do not exchange reviews with other authors or write reviews for competitors.
- No promotion: Reviews should not be used to advertise your own book or services.

- No manipulation: Reviews cannot be edited or removed in exchange for compensation.
- No insults or falsehoods: Do not post content that insults others or contains blatant falsehoods.
- No misleading content: Do not include misleading descriptions or content that doesn't accurately represent the book.

Permitted Content and Actions

- Honest opinions: Reviews should reflect your genuine opinion, whether positive or negative.
- Free or discounted copies: It is acceptable to review a free or discounted book from an author or publisher, but they cannot require a review in exchange.
- Disclosure of free copies: You must state in the review if you have received a free copy.
- Vine reviews: Reviews for free products through the Amazon
- ine program are allowed and will be labeled accordingly.
- Editorial reviews: You can pay for professional editorial reviews, which are separate from customer reviews.
- Self-editing: Reviewers can edit their own reviews after they have been posted.
- Minimum purchase: You must have spent at least $50 on Amazon in the last 12 months to be able to submit a review.

***AI: on the subject of Amazon book reviews guidelines*

Here's another article on what is permitted with Amazon Book Reviews.

*What's permitted

Amazon says this: "You may provide free or discounted copies of your books to readers. However, you may not demand a review in exchange or attempt to influence the review. Offering anything other than a free or discounted copy of the book—including gift cards—will invalidate a review, and we'll have to remove it."

Reviewers can remove or edit a review after it is posted.

Amazon says that just because a review is written by a friend or a social media connection doesn't necessarily result in that review being taken down.

A reviewer can link to another product—such as their own—if it is relevant and available on Amazon.

Friends & Family Book Reviews

A common question we hear is whether friends and family can review a book. Amazon says this: *We don't allow individuals who share a household with the author or close friends to write Customer Reviews for that author's book.*

It used to be that Amazon encouraged authors to have their friends use the customer discussions feature to promote their book. That feature has been discontinued, and readers are being referred to Goodreads Groups (requires login).

TIP: One way Amazon can monitor who your close friends are is by comparing the reviewer's contact information with the contact information in your account's address book. For example, if you've used Amazon for Christmas shopping, you probably don't want to bother asking any of those people to write a review.

Giving Books Away to Get Reviews

If you give your book away for the purpose of getting a review, you must instruct your prospective reviewer to disclose how they received your book. There are many ways for the reviewer to do this; it just must be conspicuous. They can put it at the end of the review (most common), the beginning, or in the subject line.

Here are some sample phrases you can suggest if asking others to write a review for your book.

In the subject line: *I received an ARC for an objective review.*

I received a copy of this book via [name of source, i.e., NetGalley, Edelweiss, the publisher, author] and I'm reviewing it voluntarily.

I wrote this review based on an advance reading copy that the publisher sent me.

This review was based on a complimentary pre-release copy.
https://www.authorimprints.com/amazon-book-review-policy-authors/

***How Amazon Sees It**

First off, let's be real—no one truly knows the secret sauce behind Amazon's algorithms except Amazon itself when giving out its Best Seller Rank (BSR) scoring. Their algorithms are constantly evolving, and by the time you're reading this, things could have changed again!

But from what we've observed, there's one thing that's clear: Verified Reviews carry more weight than Unverified ones when it comes to your Best Seller Rank (BSR). But this doesn't mean that unverified reviews are bad for your book. Here's a simple way to think about it: it might take five Unverified Reviews to have the same impact as one Verified Review (we're just guessing the numbers, but you get the idea!). And here's a bonus tip—reviews with photos pack an even bigger punch! It's like turning one Unverified Review into a Verified Review or one Verified Review into five. Amazon's algorithm seems to love those extra visuals because they provide more consumer confirmation that helps sell your book, and that can really help boost your BSR.

Pro Tip □

As we understand it, Amazon's algorithms not only calculate your BSR based on how many and how fast your book is selling, but also on **how frequently reviews are posted**. Sure, the first 30 days of your book launch are crucial for setting a strong BSR, but here's the kicker—if you're not getting consistent reviews (whether verified or unverified) posted at least once a week or several times a month, your BSR score could take a hit. Consistency is key to keeping Amazon's algorithms happy and your book visible!

Note: Amazon doesn't mind books receiving unverified reviews; however, Amazon does not love reviewers posting a lot of unverified reviews. Posting too many unverified reviews can affect your reviewing account.

How Consumers See It □

Now, let's talk about readers. Most consumers don't even know what a Verified Review means, let alone care about it. What they do notice is **quantity**—how many reviews does the book have? If a book has 100 reviews and another has 1000, they're probably going to gravitate towards the one with more reviews. Why? Because they'll think, "Well, if a lot of people have reviewed it, it must be good!"

Consumers usually scan products in a specific way:

- **First**: They look at how many people reviewed the book. A book with 50 reviews is more likely to beat a book with zero reviews. A book with 100 reviews is more likely to beat a book with 50 reviews. A book with 1000 reviews is more likely to beat a book with 100 reviews. Not in every case, but you get the point.
- **Next**: They check out the star rating. If it's mostly positive, great! If it's filled with 1-star and 2-star reviews, that's an immediate red flag.
- **Last**: They skim a few reviews, and trust us—they're more interested in what people didn't like than what they did like.

Important Note: Don't forget that the cover of your book, the title of your book, the interior layout and editing, and the book's selling description all play an important role in a consumer's buying decision. 98% of the time, a purchase is made from emotion.

Of course, not every shopper follows this exact pattern, but the majority do.

https://help.book-bounty.com/en/articles/9879411-verified-reviews-vs-unverified-reviews

Verified Reviews

*A Verified Review indicates the reviewer has purchased the product through the platform, such as a book bought on Amazon, which increases its credibility. An Unverified Review is from someone who acquired the product through other means, like borrowing, getting a free copy, or purchasing from a different store, and lacks this official platform confirmation. The main difference lies in the verifiable purchase history, which impacts how much trust and weight the review carries with other potential customers.

Verified Reviews

- **Indicates a purchase:** The reviewer has bought the product on the platform (e.g., Amazon) and the platform can confirm the transaction.
- **Higher credibility:** They are seen as more trustworthy because the reviewer has a confirmed, direct experience with the product.
- **Impact on ratings:** On sites like Amazon, a "Verified Purchase" badge signifies the review has more weight in the overall star rating.
- **Limitations:** The reviewer may not have purchased the item at full price, or other conditions may prevent the badge from appearing.
- Unverified Reviews
- **No confirmed purchase:** The reviewer did not buy the product through the platform where the review is posted.
- **Common sources:** These can come from people who bought the book elsewhere, received it as a gift, borrowed it from a library, or received a free copy for review.
- **Lower credibility:** These reviews are sometimes viewed with more skepticism due to the higher risk of bias or fake content since there is no verified purchase history.
- **Can still be valuable:** Despite being unverified, these reviews can still provide valuable insight into the book's quality or content.

**AI on subject of Verified Book Reviews vs. Unverified Book Reviews*

Posting Unverified Reviews to Amazon

Anyone who has spent at least $50 on Amazon in the last 12 months can submit a review, even if they didn't purchase the book on Amazon. To be eligible, the reviewer must be a real customer and not have a close financial connection to the author, such as being a family member or business partner. While the reviewer's account will not show a "Verified Purchase" badge, the review can still be helpful if it meets Amazon's community guidelines.

Who can post Unverified Reviews

- Any Amazon customer who has spent at least $50 in the last 12 months is eligible to write reviews, whether they bought the book on Amazon or elsewhere.
- Friends and family can leave reviews if they don't live with the author, share an account, or have a close financial connection with the author.
- How to post an Unverified Review
- **Log in to your Amazon account:** Sign in to the Amazon account that meets the $50 spending requirement.
- **Find the book:** Navigate to the book's page on Amazon.
- **Click "Write a product review":** You can find this option on the book's product page under the reviews section.
- **Submit your review:** Write your review and submit it. Amazon's system will check it against its community guidelines before it is posted.
- Important considerations
- **No "Verified Purchase" badge:** Unverified Reviews will not have a "Verified Purchase" badge, which can be a sign that the reviewer did not buy the product directly from Amazon.
- **Community guidelines:** The review must still comply with Amazon's community guidelines to be published.
- **Author's perspective:** While Unverified Reviews are allowed, authors are discouraged from getting too many from the same source to avoid any potential issues with their account.

Getting More Book Reviews

Book reviews provide reader credibility with the goal of converting visitors into buyers of your title. There are two types of formal book reviews:

Editorial Review

Editorial Review is where a professional third party gives an unbiased critique of your work. Their comments relate to structure, style, or merit. These reviews come from book editors, trade publications, and experts in the genre. They are used to educate the audience on new books.
Free editorial reviews:
Midwest Book Review
Booklist by American Library Assn.
Library Journal
City Book Review
Washington Independent Review of Books
Porchlight Books
Reader's Favorite
Reader's View

Paid Review

Paid Review is when the title is submitted with the goal of increasing exposure, finding readers, and bumping the review count. According to the Amazon contract, it is not legal to pay for a book review. The way the companies get around it is they charge the authors to post their book, then show it to a specified audience who reads it (for free), with the hope they will leave a review. Some boast of high review numbers based on history. Here is an overview of some of the largest book review options.

Book Sirens- They offer paid plans of $10 per month with a reader plan of $2 per book.
How it works: The author submits a book. If it is accepted, then it is added to a bank of similar books and shown to readers (who have been vetted). They promote it for three months. When someone downloads the book, the subscriber is charged $2. You cannot remove bad reviews.

They are honest and unbiased.
Book Sirens does not pay readers for reviews, but the $ is for them to locate readers. Authors can invite readers to join the review team. Negative reviews cannot be removed. The reviews are honest and unbiased. Authors may request reviews be posted to Amazon, Kobo, Apple, Book Hub and Google.

Booksprouts.com
NetGalley is a company that connects book publishers with reviewers, often from media, libraries, and book sellers. Subscribers pay for them to post the book, which is put out on their database of readers. They release ARCs (Advanced Reading Copies) to their database.
This is a good option for the prelaunch of a book.
These are not typical readers, but those with education and expertise in the field.
Database includes those from Australia, Canada, France, Germany, Japan, UK and USA
Reviewers are critics and may not leave 5-star reviews.
Cost is $849 per title or $495 for 6 months. Can join for lower cost by joining IBPA or Xpress Services.
Those submitting books have access to reader profiles and can approve or disapprove of allowing them to read their book.
Book review comparisons…per AI online
Book review options can be categorized by purpose, including social platforms like Goodreads for reader engagement, professional services like NetGalley for pre-publication exposure, and sites like Book Marks that aggregate professional critics' opinions. Other options include paid review services, but it's important to distinguish these from legitimate editorial reviews, as paid reviews can vary widely in quality and verifiability. Academic or comparative reviews, on the other hand, are a different type of writing that requires comparing two or more books in depth.

For Readers

Goodreads:
A social platform where users can track reading, write reviews, and connect with other readers and authors.

Book Marks:
Aggregates professional book reviews from various major publications, providing an average grade for a book.

Academic/Comparative Reviews:
Written pieces that critically compare two or more books, often for a course or a personal project.

Grammarly Blog:
Offers guidance on writing a personal book review, focusing on plot, character, pacing, and literary devices.

For Authors

NetGalley:
A service for authors to get pre-publication digital copies of their book to reviewers in exchange for feedback and reviews.

Book Bounty/Book Reverb:
These are services that can be used to obtain verified book reviews, though the quality and authenticity can vary. They are a way to supplement other review strategies.

ACX (Audiobook Creation Exchange) and Reedsy:
Other platforms where authors can find reviewers and services, though the pay varies.

Paid review services:
Services like EssayHub offer paid book review writing assistance, though they differ from professional editorial reviews.

How to Choose the Right Option

For Readers:

Choose Goodreads for social interaction and personal discovery. Use Book Marks to see professional critical opinions. Opt for comparative reviews when a deep analysis is required.

For Authors:

Choose NetGalley for a professional and established pre-publication reviewer community. Consider using paid review services to supplement your review strategy but be mindful of the quality and verifiability of the reviews. You may need to use a combination of services to achieve your desired results.

Book Reviews

A Great New Tool for Getting More Book Reviews on Amazon (video)

https://www.youtube.com/watch?v=xpektAEf39E

Summary of Video:

Did you know that signing up for multiple review services could kill your Amazon account—even if your intentions are good? In this episode of BookLaunchers.tv, Julie Broad, founder of Book Launchers, breaks down the right way to ethically grow your Amazon reviews using GetBooksReviewed.com, a community-driven, token-based platform that helps authors earn authentic reviews the Amazon-approved way.

Julie Broad and Book Launchers' book marketing expert Sarah Bean tested this platform with several client books to find out: Does it actually work? How fast can you realistically earn verified reviews? And is it safe from Amazon's tightening review policies in 2025? Our affiliate link for Get Books Reviewed, if you want to check it out, is: https://www.booklaunchers.com/gbr

In this video on getting book reviews on Amazon, you'll learn:

□ Why using multiple review services can put your account at risk.

□ How Get Books Reviewed's token system keeps reviews ethical and compliant.

□ What makes their new Friends & Family Network feature a game-changer.

□ The difference between verified and unverified reviews—and why it

matters.
□ How to pace your review growth safely (and what bonuses actually work).
□ The latest Amazon guideline twist that could affect every author in 2025.
If you've ever tried BookSirens, BookSprout, or Goodreads Giveaways, you'll want to see how this one compares. Spoiler: it's not perfect, but it's promising—and Julie shares exactly what worked and what didn't.

Videos

1
0 Sites to get More Book Reviews
https://www.youtube.com/watch?v=SVp1LCYZ7kk
Getting Book Reviews with BookSprout and BookSirens
https://www.youtube.com/watch?v=sWKsNix3hK0
What's Worked to Get More Book Reviews
https://www.youtube.com/watch?v=H4-lsNOZcnE
Best Paid Book Review Sites for Authors
https://www.youtube.com/watch?v=1uOlNf9Bdeo
Getting Book Reviews with NetGalley
https://www.youtube.com/watch?v=MpnTsFYg8hA
Why Every Author Needs a Goodreads Account
https://www.youtube.com/watch?v=cRTCwBkeess

Christian Book Marketing 2026

Section 1 General Book Marketing
Section 2 Selling Christian Books
Section 3 Target Marketing
Section 4 Avenues of Marketing
Section 5 Recognizing a Marketing Scam
Section 6 Book Reviews
Section 7 Selling Used Books
- Best Apps for Used and Textbook Value
- Best Apps for Rare and Collectible Books
- Seller Central

Section 8 Book Awards
Section 9 Develop a Book Launch Plan

Section 7 →

Selling Used Books

Selling Used Books

*AI Google data
Several apps like BookScouter and BookTrapper can tell you the value of a used book by scanning its barcode or ISBN to compare prices from different vendors. For rare or collectible books, tools like Book-Boss and Collector's Chronicle use AI and past auction data to estimate their value.

Best Apps for Used and Textbook Value

BookScouter: Allows you to scan a book's barcode or ISBN to see prices from over 30 different buyback vendors. You can then choose the vendor with the best offer.

BookTrapper: Another app for iOS and Android that lets you scan barcodes or enter ISBNs to compare book prices from multiple sources.

Ziffit: A simple app that provides an instant selling price for a book when you scan the barcode, which you can then sell directly through the app.

Best Apps for Rare and Collectible Books

BookBoss: An upcoming tool that uses past auction sale data and artificial intelligence to estimate the value of rare books.

Collector's Chronicle: A free app that uses AI to help identify and appraise books, providing potential value and historical information.

Seller Central

*AI Google Search Data
To sell books through Seller Central on Amazon, first create a seller account, then list books by finding them in the Amazon catalog using the ISBN, title, or by scanning the barcode with the Seller App. After finding the book, click "sell this product," select the condition, set a price, and choose your fulfillment method (FBA or FBM) to complete the listing.

1. **Set up your account**

2. **Sign up:** Create an Amazon seller account on sell.amazon.com.

3. **Choose a plan:** Decide between an Individual plan (best for fewer than 40 sales/month) or a Professional plan (more cost-effective for high-volume sellers).

4. **List your books**

5. **Find the book:** In Seller Central or the Amazon Seller App, go to "Add Products" and search for the book.

6. **ISBN or ASIN:** The fastest method is to scan the barcode or enter the book's ISBN (International Standard Book Number) or ASIN (Amazon Standard Identification Number).

7. **Manual search:** If you can't find it by ISBN/ASIN, search for the book by its title, especially if it was published before 1970 and doesn't have an ISBN.

8. **Create the listing:** Once the book's page is found, click "Sell this product."

9. **Select condition:** Choose the condition of your book (e.g., new, used).

10. **Set price:** Enter a competitive price for your listing.

11. **Add details:** Write a compelling title and description to help your book stand out.

12. **Choose your fulfillment method.**

13. **Fulfillment by Amazon (FBA):** You can ship your books in bulk to an Amazon fulfillment center, and Amazon will handle storage, packing, and shipping for you.

14. **Fulfillment by Merchant (FBM):** You are responsible for packing and shipping the books to customers yourself after they place an order.

Christian Book Marketing 2026

Section 1 General Book Marketing
Section 2 Selling Christian Books
Section 3 Target Marketing
Section 4 Avenues of Marketing
Section 5 Recognizing a Marketing Scam
Section 6 Book Reviews
Section 7 Selling Used Books
Section 8 Book Awards
- Awards for Self-Published Books
- Awards for Unpublished Manuscripts
- Awards for Traditionally Published Books
- Genre Specific Awards

Section 9 Develop a Book Launch Plan

Section 8 →

Book Awards

Awards for Self-Published Books

1. The IndieReader Discovery Awards
The IndieReader Discovery Awards feature distinctions such as "Best First Book," "Best Cover Design," and overall best fiction and nonfiction, as well as winners from each genre. The judges read all submissions and recommend the top six winners to Dystel, Goderich & Bourret for representation. The winners receive cash and other prizes based on the category won.
Who can win? Self-published, hybrid, and small press–published authors, in either e-book or paper book format.
When can you submit? Annually; the deadline is typically in February.
Entry fee: $150 for the first entry; an additional $50 per category entered.

2. The Independent Publisher Book Awards
Sponsored by Independent Publisher since 1996, the "IPPY" Awards are open to any independent author or publisher worldwide who produces books intended for an English-speaking audience. They award gold, silver, and bronze medals to winners in over 100 categories.
Who can win? Self-published authors, independent publishers, university presses.
When can you submit? Annually; the deadline is typically in March.
Entry fee: Ranges from the early bird fee of $79 to $99 closer to the deadline.

3. The Foreword INDIES Book of the Year Award
The Foreword INDIES Book Awards, sponsored by *Foreword Reviews*, was established in 1998 to promote indie books and small presses to the magazine's large audience of librarians and booksellers. The top two winners each receive a $1,500 cash prize and are promoted with the

other finalists through press releases, events, articles, and social media to *Foreword*'s list of over 35,000+ industry connections.
Who can apply? Self-published authors, independent publishers, and university presses, in print or e-book format.
When can you submit? Annually; the deadline is typically in January.
Entry fee: $119 per title for the first category; $99 for subsequent categories.

4. The Next Generation Indie Book Awards
Drawing from more than 80 categories, the Next Generation Indie Book Awards is the largest international awards program for indies. They offer $1,500 to the first-place winner and smaller cash prizes to runners-up and finalists in each category. In addition, New York literary agent Marilyn Allen of the Allen Literary Agency considers the top books for publication.
Who can win? Self-published authors, independent publishers, and university presses.
When can you submit? Annually; the deadline is typically in February.
Entry fee: $80 per title for the first category; $65 for subsequent categories.

5. The Best Indie Book Award
The "BIBA" is a self-sponsored award with contests for the best books in 35 categories, as well as for best illustration and best cover design. These contests are open to authors all over the world, including those published with very small presses! Winners receive a trophy and ongoing promotion to BIBA's 100,000+ followers. In addition, BIBA selects one Book of the Year from the winners to receive a cash prize of $2,000.
Who can win? Self-published authors, independent and hybrid publishers, and university presses.
When can you submit? Annually; submissions open on January 1 and close mid-August each year.
Entry fee: $75 per title per category for the literary award ($60 for early entry); $60 per entry for the illustration and cover design awards.

6. The National Indie Excellence Awards
The National Indie Excellence Awards recognize authors and publishers who "produce books of excellence in every aspect." They select overall

winners and also several finalists for each category, with sponsor prizes and cash prizes of $500 up for grabs.
Who can win? Small presses, midsize independent publishers, university presses, and self-published authors. *Note:* Only print books may be entered, not e-books.
When can you submit? Annually; the submission timeframe typically runs from August to March.
Entry fee: $75 per book per category.

7. Eric Hoffer Book Award
The Eric Hoffer Book Award has honored independent books for more than two decades in memory of its namesake. It offers a grand prize of $5,000 to one recipient each year, as well as worldwide media exposure and coverage in the *US Review of Books*. The award also gives category prizes and honors for the best presses, the most thought-provoking books, exceptional cover art, and more.
Who can win? Self-published authors, academic presses, and small/micro presses.
When can you submit? Annually; the deadline is typically in January each year.
Entry fee: $60 per entry for early registration; $75 thereafter; $45 for eligible books with 40 pages or less.

8. Writer's Digest Self-Published Book Awards
Writer's Digest holds two competitions for books. The self-published e-book award honors one grand prize winner (across genres) with $5,000 in cash, while the self-published print book award offers a grand prize of $10,000. Both competitions also award the grand prize winner a featured interview in their magazine, publication of an excerpt of the winning book on their website, and a paid trip to the *Writer's Digest* Annual Conference! Winning first prize in each category isn't shabby either, with an award of $1,000 in cash and a press announcement. All e-book award entrants also receive a review from one of *Writer's Digest*'s annual writing competition readers.
Self-Published Book Awards
Who can win? Self-published authors who have paid the full cost of publication, or whose cost of printing was paid for by a grant or as part of a prize.
When can you submit? Annually. The deadline is typically May 1,

with an early bird deadline of April 1.
Entry fee: $125 for the first entry, $110 for each additional entry; the early bird fee is $100 for the first entry, $85 for each additional entry.
Self-Published E-book Awards
Who can win? Self-published authors of e-books published in the past five years; authors who publish with a small press that publishes fewer than 12 e-books a year; authors who have traditionally published in print but retained their e-book rights.
When can you submit? Annually. The deadline is typically mid-September, with an early bird deadline of mid-August.
Entry fee: $125 for the first entry, $110 for each additional entry; the early-bird fee is $100 for the first entry, $85 for each additional entry.

9. Rubery Book Awards
The Rubery Book Awards are a UK-based international book award offering one grand "Book of the Year" prize and £2,000 in cash. Smaller cash prizes are also awarded to category winners. The judges accept books in all categories and decide which categories to represent after receiving all entries.
Who can win? Self-published authors and independent presses, in print or e-book format, with no publication date restriction.
When can you submit? Annually; the deadline is typically March 31. Entries submitted after this date are automatically entered into the following year's award.
Entry fee: £45 / $70.

Awards for Unpublished Manuscripts

10. Autumn House Fiction Prize
The Autumn House Fiction Prize is unique in that it honors books that haven't been published yet. If you're sitting on a manuscript between 150 and 300 pages, consider submitting it to this annual prize. Autumn House offers one winner a book contract for publication and $2,500 in cash, and they also consider all finalists for publication.
Who can win? All authors whose submitted manuscripts are unpublished. *Note:* Only fiction (and subgenres of fiction) are considered for this prize, but Autumn House also offers a Nonfiction Prize and a Rising Writer Prize for poetry.

When can you submit? Annually; the submission period typically runs from January 1 through the end of February.
Entry fee: $35, waived for those undergoing financial hardship.

Awards for Traditionally Published Books

11. National Book Awards
Each year, the National Book Foundation assembles 25 esteemed judges to vote on the best book of the year in the United States. They currently recognize the best Fiction, Nonfiction, Poetry, Translated Literature, and Young People's Literature. Five finalists from each category receive a cash prize of $1,000, and the winner from each category, announced at the highly anticipated annual awards ceremony, receives $10,000!
Who can win? US authors nominated by their publishing house are eligible to win all awards except the Translated Literature Award, which doesn't require the author or translator to be a US citizen. *Note:* Self-published books are eligible if the author or publisher also publishes the work of other authors.
When can you submit? Annually; the submission period typically runs each March through May.
Entry fee: $135 per title.

12. The Encore Award
First presented in 1990 and now facilitated by the Royal Society of Literature, the Encore Award honors outstanding second novels of the year. The annual winner of this UK-based award receives a prize of £15,000.
Who can win? UK publishers may submit books published in the current calendar year. Translated works, novellas, and children's books are ineligible.
When can you submit? Annually; the deadline is typically in January.
Entry fee: Free.

13. Women's Prize for Fiction
First awarded in 1996 as a reaction to the all-male 1991 Booker Prize shortlist, the Women's Prize for Fiction annually honors exceptional books by women writers. The winner receives £30,000. Run by

the Women's Prize Trust, a charity focused on creating equitable opportunities for women in publishing, the prize is considered one of the UK's most prestigious literary awards.
Who can win? Women authors writing in English. UK publishers must submit books for consideration; authors may not submit their own books.
When can you submit? Submission dates are staggered based on publication date. Find the latest terms and conditions for entry on the website.
Entry fee: Publishers are required to make different financial contributions for books that are longlisted, shortlisted, or selected as winners. See the terms and conditions for entry.

14. The Booker Prize
Since 1969, the Booker Prize has been awarded annually to an outstanding work of fiction published in the UK, with the winner receiving £50,000, and £2,500 awarded to shortlisted authors. Being included on the longlist for this prize is a distinct honor as well, drawing international attention. See also: The International Booker Prize.
Who can win? Any novel originally written in English and published in the UK and Ireland in the year of the prize is eligible. Only publishers can submit entries.
When can you submit? Submission dates are tiered based on publication date. Find the latest terms and conditions for entry on the website.
Entry fee: Publishers are no longer required to make a financial contribution if their book is shortlisted or selected to win.

15. PEN Open Book Award
Among other literary awards like the Emerging Writers Prize and the PEN/Voelcker Award for Poetry, PEN America sponsors the PEN Open Book Award, which celebrates and honors exceptional books published by authors of color. The winner receives a cash prize of $10,000 as well as a fully funded residency at Civitella!
Who can win? Authors of color who have not received wide media coverage. Publishers or literary agents must handle the submission process; authors may not submit their own books.
When can you submit? Annually; submissions typically open in June and close in August.
Entry fee: $85.

16. The PEN/Faulkner Award for Fiction
As well as awards for debut novels, short stories, and literary advocacy, The PEN/Faulkner Foundation honors the best works of fiction across genres each year. The winner receives $15,000, and the five finalists each receive $5,000, presented at an annual awards celebration.
Who can win? Traditionally published US authors. Publishers or literary agents must submit entries; authors may not submit their own books.
When can you submit? Annually; the submission period typically runs from July 1 through September 30.
Entry fee: $95.

17. The Pulitzer Prize
This prestigious prize hardly needs an introduction, but what you may not know is that anyone (including the author) can submit a book for consideration. Each year, Columbia University awards Pulitzer Prizes for books in six categories, including genre fiction, of $15,000 each. Winners are chosen by the Pulitzer Prize Board, which recently expanded the citizenship requirements: The awards are now open to non-US citizens.
Who can win? Authors living in the US (including non-citizens) whose submitted book was published in English and in the US, and preferably deals with American life. Both authors and publishers may make entries. *Note:* Self-published books are eligible if the book is also published in print format by a US-based press.
When can you submit? Annually; the recommended deadline depends on publication year. Check the website for the latest information.
Entry fee: $75

Genre-Specific Awards

18. Horror: Shirley Jackson Awards
Established in 2007 in recognition of its namesake's legacy, the Shirley Jackson Awards honor "outstanding achievements" in the horror, psychological suspense, and dark fantasy genres. The awards, presented at the annual Readercon conference, are given in six categories, including novel, novella, and anthology. Previous winners include Stephen King and Karen Russell!
Who can win? Authors of works with elements of horror, psychological suspense, or dark fantasy. *Note:* Only editors or publishers may submit works to the jury for consideration.
When can you submit? Annually; check the award rules for submission dates.
Entry fee: None, but you can support the awards with a donation.

19. Horror: Bram Stoker Awards
The Horror Writers Association presents the Bram Stoker Awards across categories such as Young Adult, First Novel, Anthology, and more for "superior achievement" in dark fantasy and horror writing. Authors and publishers may submit books, or members of the HWA may nominate books for consideration.
Who can win? Both self-published and traditionally published authors writing in the horror genre.
When can you submit? The final deadline is November 30 each year.
Entry fee: Free.

20. Science Fiction and Fantasy: Locus Awards
The Locus Awards were originally inaugurated by the science fiction and fantasy magazine *Locus* to predict the Hugo Awards through an annual reader poll. Now, unlike other science fiction and fantasy awards, voting is open online to anyone, not just the magazine's subscribers. And there's no specific submission process for the Locus Awards; rather, you go through the submission process for review consideration. Ten finalists in 17 categories are celebrated at the Locus Awards ceremony in California.
Who can win? Authors of science fiction, fantasy, horror, speculative, surreal, slipstream, crossed genres, similarly themed YA, art books, and

related nonfiction.
When can you submit? Anytime; the voting deadline is April 15 each year.
Entry fee: Free.

21. LGBTQ+: Lambda Literary Awards
The "Lammys" have celebrated queer literary excellence for over three decades! These awards honor more than 150 writers across 26 categories — each judged by a panel of selected readers and authors, including former finalists — at an annual awards ceremony in New York City. In addition to the Lammys, Lambda Literary gives cash prizes for "outstanding contributions made by individuals to LGBTQ+ literature, culture, and community."
Who can win? Self-published authors and traditionally published authors, regardless of sexual orientation or gender identity. Works reflecting identities beyond LGBTQ+ or questioning are also welcome, but should be relevant to LGBTQ+ lives.
When can you submit? Annually; submissions are open between September and November.
Entry fee: $115 for Big Five publishers and universities; for small presses/independent publishers and indie authors, the fee is $65 per title for 1-10 titles and $55 per title for 11+ titles.

22. BIPOC: Coretta Scott King Book Awards
Named for Coretta Scott King to honor her work continuing her husband Martin Luther King Jr.'s legacy, this award recognizes "outstanding inspirational and educational" books by Black authors for children and young adults. The American Library Association (ALA) announces the winning authors and illustrators at the annual Youth Media Awards.
Who can win? African American authors and illustrators of books reflecting the African American experience.
When can you submit? The deadline each year is December 31.
Entry fee: Free.

23. BIPOC: NAACP Literary Image Award
The NAACP Image Awards recognize the outstanding achievements of people of color in film, TV, music, podcasting, and literature. The nine Literary categories include best fiction, nonfiction, debut author, and the newly added best graphic novel. The star-studded annual awards cere-

mony airs on BET and CBS in March.
Who can win? Authors and illustrators who meet the requirements for each category — you can see the latest submission guidelines on the website when submissions are open.
When can you submit? Annually; the deadline is typically in November.
Entry fee: $400 per submission, with an additional $50 fee to ship physical books.

24. BIPOC: Zora Awards (formerly Legacy Awards)
In April 2025, the Hurston/Wright Foundation's Legacy Awards were rebranded as the Zora Awards, in tribute to Zora Neale Hurston, one of the preeminent writers of African-American literature. The "Zoras" honor excellence by Black writers across four major categories: Fiction, Debut Fiction, Nonfiction, and Poetry. The rebranding introduced a larger cash prize for the Debut Fiction winner of $20,000!
Who can win? Self-published or traditionally published Black writers in the United States and globally. Books may be submitted by the author, publisher, or literary agent.
When can you submit? Submissions open the day after the annual awards ceremony in October and close at the end of the year.
Entry fee: Free.

25. Jewish Interest: National Jewish Book Awards
The National Jewish Book Awards, presented annually by the Jewish Book Council since 1950, are the longest-running literary awards program of their kind. These awards recognize exceptional Jewish literature across a wide range of genres to preserve and celebrate Jewish culture and heritage.
Who can win? Self-published, traditionally published, and unpublished authors (manuscripts are eligible) of books with Jewish content. All books, including e-books, must be submitted in print format, and may be submitted by the author or publisher.
When can you submit? Annually; the deadline is typically in September.
Entry fee: $170 per title.

26. Western: Spur Awards
Presented by the Western Writers of America (WWA), the Spur Awards honor distinguished writing about the American West across 18 categories, including western traditional, historical, contemporary, and

romance. Winners and finalists are invited to the annual WWA Convention, where winners receive a plaque at the Spur Awards banquet, and finalists receive a certificate.
Who can win? Self-published and traditionally published authors of works set in or related to the American West or the frontier experience. All books, including e-books, must be submitted in print format and may be submitted by the author or publisher.
When can you submit? These awards have two submission deadlines based on the date of publication. You can find the schedule on the website.
Entry fee: Free.

27. Children's: Newbery Medal
Operating since 1922, the John Newbery Medal is the world's oldest continuing award for distinguished children's books. The award lends much prestige to the winning book of the year, which receives wide media coverage and interest from bookstores and libraries. The Association for Library Service to Children, a division of the ALA, awards the medal at the annual Youth Media Awards.
Who can win? Any US author (self-published or traditionally published) whose book is intended for children up to age 14.
When can you submit? The deadline each year is December 31.
Entry fee: Free.

28. Christian Fiction: The Christy Awards
Named for Catherine Marshall's bestselling novel *Christy,* the Christy Awards have honored excellence in fiction written from a Christian worldview since 1991. The Evangelical Christian Publishers Association presents these awards annually, selecting a winner from each of its nine categories.
Who can win? Traditionally published authors of books with a Christian worldview. Self-published authors are also eligible if they meet certain requirements.
When can you submit? Annually; the submission period is March 1 to March 31.
Entry fee: $175.

29. Christian Fiction: Carol Awards
American Christian Fiction Writers (ACFW) established the Carol

Awards to recognize the best Christian fiction across 11 categories. These categories are similar to the Christy Awards, but also include best romantic suspense, novella, and debut novel.
Who can win? Traditionally published authors of books written from a Christian worldview, in print or e-book format. Self-published authors who meet certain criteria are also eligible. *Note:* Only authors may enter; publishers may not enter for their authors.
When can you submit? Annually; the next submission period runs from January 2 to March 1.
Entry fee: $50 per entry for ACFW members; $135 per entry for non-members.

30. Political Writing: Orwell Prize
The Orwell Foundation presents this annual award, named after the acclaimed author of *1984*, George Orwell, to honor exceptional fictional and nonfiction works that "make political writing into an art." The book prizes for Political Fiction and Political Writing each award £3,000 to the winner.
Who can win? Traditionally published books, which must be submitted by their publishing house, that were first published in the UK.
When can you submit? Annually; submissions are typically open from November to January. Find the latest schedule here.
Entry fee: Shortlisted publishers are required to pay £750 toward promotional costs.

31. Mystery: Edgar Awards
Mystery Writers of America presents the Edgar Awards annually to celebrate mystery books. Named in honor of Edgar Allen Poe, the Edgar Awards have multiple subgenres, such as short stories, young adult, true crime, and more. They are largely regarded as the most prestigious award in the genre!
Who can win? Traditionally published authors writing in the mystery/thriller genre who meet the Active Status membership requirements. Books can be submitted by the publisher or the author.
When can you submit? These awards operate on a tiered submission schedule based on the date of publication throughout the year. See the schedule here.
Entry fee: Free.

32. Crime Writing: The CWA Daggers

Aptly named for their genre, the CWA Daggers are annual awards given for excellence in UK crime fiction and nonfiction by the Crime Writers' Association. There are several Daggers (or competitions) for books that publishers and authors can enter, ranging from the Gold Dagger for the best crime novel to the Emerging Author Dagger, open to unpublished authors around the world.

Who can win? Traditionally published authors, as well as self-published authors who are members of the CWA. Both authors and CWA-approved publishers can nominate books for consideration.

When can you submit? These awards have two submission deadlines based on the date of publication. See the schedule here.

Entry fee: £75 per title (half the regular fee for CWA members).

Christian Book Marketing 2026

Section 1 General Book Marketing
Section 2 Selling Christian Books
Section 3 Target Marketing
Section 4 Avenues of Marketing
Section 5 Recognizing a Marketing Scam
Section 6 Book Reviews
Section 7 Selling Used Books
Section 8 Book Awards
Section 9 Develop a Book Launch Plan

- Book Inventory
- Make a Page
- Sample Book Launch Marketing Plan
- Glorybound Publishing Book Launch Assessment
- Book Launch Marketing Plan Details
- Book Marketplace Net
- Book Market Mania
- Book Marketing Videos

Section 9 →

Develop a Book Launch Plan

Book Inventory

Many authors come to me looking for a marketing plan when they already have several books, with more in process. It is important to begin with an inventory of the books, their formats and existing marketing before launching out with a new plan. The new plan needs to connect to an existing plan for the best results. Think of it like this; you are not going to launch out and make new friends when you release a book in a series. It is better to tell those who have purchased the first one that the next one is ready to read!

To begin with figure out what you have (already).

List each book independently under the title

Each book title

- List the title
- ISBN
- Publisher
- Date of Publication
- Volume #
- Contributors
- Where the book can be purchased
- Is the copyright registered with the US Copyright? When?

· Format of the book (paperback, hardbound, audio, Kindle)

· Adjunct options with this book (video, trailer, banner, cards)

If there are several books, are they part of a series?

· Title of series

· Volumes included in the series

Are there books not yet published (or formats) to follow?

· Title

· Are they related to other published books?

We make a single page for authors with several books that shows exactly what is going on with that book. You can make as many columns as needed. Having the cover and summary are helpful. It makes it easy to see how the books compare with one another.

Make a Page

When People Came Series						
Volume		**Size**	**Info**	**Hard-bound**	**Paper-back**	**Kin-dle-E**
Vol 1-Summary 5-24-25		8.5 x 11, Full-color 161 pg, 173 photos. Matte Cvr	**ISBN**	4000	4003	4004
			Print $	13.53	11.96	0
			Retail $	25.00	16.00	6.99
			Royalty	2.47	2.49	
Vol 2-Summary 5-24-25		8.5 x 11, Full-color 194 pg, 187 photos. Matte Cvr	**ISBN**	4001	4005	4006
			Print $	13.53	11.96	0
			Retail $	25.00	16.00	6.99
			Royalty	2.23	4.48	
Vol 3-Summary 5-24-25		8.5 x 11, Full-color 236 pages, 284 photos Matte Cvr	**ISBN**	4007	4008	4009
			Print $	13.53	11.96	0
			Retail $	25.00	16.00	6.99
			Royalty	1.87	2.92	

Sample Book Launch Marketing Plan

Below is a sample Book Launch Marketing Plan. The author had two books previously published and was coming to me to assist in publishing the third book of a series. We published the third of the series and then went on to enact the marketing plan.

Trilogy of Books

1. Maximize the books
2. On Line presence (unify your face)
3. Ivorymind summary
4. Increase the book reviews 50
5. Author press release
6. Qr Codes
7. Shortened URL
8. Business cards / foam board
9. Bookmarket Mania

We began the marketing plan by looking over the previously published books and running them through a process of making sure their embedded keywords and summaries were solid. He wanted the book covers changed, so we put that on the list. We serialized the books on KDP and Amazon so they will help to market each other when they are displayed.

We made fresh Kindle E Books using the latest software to ensure they were market ready.

Then we coached him in obtaining the best book reviews and showed him how to release emails to his followers telling them of his books.

We made a press release which included all three of the series providing a full-page, two per page PDF so he can print them when he attends events. Then we made a JPG so he can use it on his wife's Facebook page. He said she was the main user of Facebook and willing to flash his book around.

We located the link on Amazon where his book is sold and used Tinylink app to shorten the link. This was helpful for his marketing campaign. Then we obtained a QR code to the location of his book.

He wanted some business cards with the QR code and cover of the book, so we ordered a box from Vistaprint and had them delivered to his house. He did not have an author website, so we recommended he come aboard the Bookmarketplace.Net and put his books on the book marketing websites (we own). They are high traffic websites. We put up to 3 books by one author on 2 sites for $10 per month.

Glorybound Publishing Book Launch Assessment

Glorybound Publishing
439 S. 6th St. Camp Verde, AZ 86322
PH 928-567-3340

www.gloryboundpublishing.com
sheri@gloryboundpublishing.com

Glorybound Publishing

Glorybound Publishing
Breathing life into dreams and dreams into books

mania2026

Christian Book mania 2026

Author Name: Phone:
Email:
Title of Work:
NOTES:

Book Launch Cost & Time Assessment

→Book Launch [office and on-line]

- ☐ **Book Marketing Consultation [inc book launch timeline]** ________

- ☐ **a. Author Central w unique URL** ________
- ☐ **b. US Copyright Registration** + US fee $65 ________
- ☐ **c. Key Word Optimization (metadata)** ________
- ☐ **d. Comprehensive AI Book Summary** ________
- ☐ **e. Key words & Photo Object Export Options into Files** ________
- ☐ **f. Kindle E Book (include c-e)** ________
- ☐ **g. Locate URL, shorten, and make a QR Code** ________
- ☐ **h. Book Review Coaching** ________
- ☐ **i. Author Press Release** ________
- ☐ **j. Email Marketing Plan** ________
- ☐ **k. Set up a Free Book Promotion** ________

→Live Marketing

- ☐ **l. Order business cards, banner, foam board** ________
- ☐ **m. Square-up account** ________
- ☐ **n. Author recorded interview** ________
- ☐ **o. Bookstores and event sales** ________
- ☐ **p. Marketplace Website Advertisement** ________
- ☐ **q. Amazon pay-per-click Ad** ________

Sub-total ________
TAX [10%] ________
Total: ________

Book Launch Marketing Plan Details

Adding Value to the book

Author Central with unique URL

Author.amazon.com to fill out author central: Once an author publishes a book on Amazon he/she has an option of having an author page.

- Set up dedicated URL with author name to help locate the author on Amazon
- Bio photograph
- Biograph with followers on Amazon
- Sets up an option to respond to book reviews

US Copyright Registration

Register copyright with the US Copyright Office (3 months after publication)

- Registration of the copyright helps to preserve author credibility.
- Provides legal recourse for potential incursion of copyright.
- Involves setting up an account with the US Copyright and paying the fee to the copyright office ($65).

Ivorymind summary of each book

Book Summary (Ivorymind). It is important to have a complete simple summary of the book. The summary is used in many areas of sales. We use a software to help generate a clean summary.

- One paragraph
- Clean language
- Precise wording
- Depict the entire book from start to finish

Sample Book Reviews and Coaching (3)

Book reviews are key to selling books on-line because they add buyer confidence and credibility to the product. The goal is to obtain honest high-value reviews. See the video on Book Market Mania website on Book Reviews Good, Better and Best for more information on the best quality of book reviews.

- We assist authors in understanding the value of book reviews and write several to get them going.
- Demonstrate how to post a book review for their book—by posting a valued book review on their site.

Keywords

Book Optimization. Maximize book searchability helps readers to locate the book. Key Words (metadata) is used on websites. A website is similar to a quilt—the reader sees the front of the site while the strings on the backside provide access for web search engines to know what is on the website. Many websites add metadata separately to ensure readers locate their website when seeking specific services or products. It is called 'website optimization' when used in web design. We use it in book promotion to help readers find the book. Key words are located and inserted within the files while producing the book body and cover giving the book greater weight on line. When the book is shown on line, the key words go along with it. Therefore if key words are embedded in the body and in the cover, the key words are twice, giving double advantage of helping the customer to locate the book title.

- KDP Rocket is the software used to ascertain the best key words for marketing. Software will locate words most frequently typed in that are used for the specific subject of the book. One person may look for a children's book typing in the phrase, "books for 4 year-olds," while another may type in the phrase, "dog books for kids."
  The first phrase has 120 searches per month with $340 in sales. The second phrase has 450 searches per month with $2300 in sales. Therefore, it is better to use the phrase "dog books for kids" instead of "books for 4 year-olds" because it will generate more views thus more sales. That is the power of key words.
- Select word phrases which most accurately depict the subject of the book AND generate the most potential sales.
- Select 20-30 word phrases per book.

Photo Object Export Options

Photo Object Export Options help vision impaired with photo identification.

- Identify the photos and give short descriptions to provide reader optimization for use in the on-line version of the book.

- Tags photos and ensures copyright of pictures as needed.
- Helps to professionalize the book and elevate standards of publication.

E Books with Kindle Create
Kindle E Book: Ensure the e-book is the best edition for maximum readability related to book content.

- Kindle-E Book in modern format: Reflowable, comic, kids, or print replica on Kindle Create
- Key Words embedded into the file
- *Ivorymind* Summary embedded into the file
- Photo Object Export (identifying all photos)
- Table of Contents

URL with URL shortener and QR Code
Locate the URL (Uniform Resource Locator) is the web address of where the book is located. It may be an author website, sales website, or directly on Amazon where the book is posted. The URL can be copied directly from the website from the top. It is often over 4 lines long and can be intimidating to follow. We have found that, by shortening the URL it makes the link much easier to manage. We use a service to shorten the link.

- Shorten the URL to a manageable size. We use a service called TinyURL.
- Make a QR Code. The QR code is usable for paper flyers, business cards and promotional media. Potential buyers can scan the QR code with their phone and are directed straight to purchasing the book.
  *Note—a QR code made from a short link is less dense than one from a long link and is easier for QR Code Readers to follow.

Author Press Release
An author press release is a single piece of paper useful live and on-line. We make page size, then two per page (so author can print and bring to live events) and Jpeg with live links that can be put on-line on social media, websites, and text.

- Book cover

- Book Summary
- Author photo
- Author biography
- QR Code of the book
- Author contact information

E-mail list of followers (people interested in your success).
Email list and letter. We generate a sample email that authors can send to their followers.

- We show authors how to make an e-mail list of their friends and followers attaching the author press release and embedding the shortened url of the book.
- Recommend 50 as a starting number of emails to gather.

Timeline of free 5-day book Release 2 per year
Free Book Promotion. Free book promotions are limited to Kindle E Books which are released on KDP.

When is a good time to release the book for free?

How to release the book. (See video on BookMarketMania website)

Fill in template email for each book with summary, url, sample book review.
The template which is provided to send the email followers can be filled in by Glorybound with all of the information. This makes it easy for authors to send them at specific times just prior to the release of the book and when it is offered for free.

E-mail includes:

- Ivorymind summary
- A plea for reading the book and providing a book review
- Shortened URL link to go straight to the book on Amazon
- Sample book review
- Directions on how to leave a book review.

*Education and help with additional book review option are available on https://bookmarketmania.com

Add QR Code on business card with cover and order
The QR code is can be added to one side of the business card on the right side and the book cover on the left side. These are a quick way to send others to the book for purchase. May add the Free Book dates to the cards as well and have them ready to hand out. Dates can be set ahead of time on KDP.

- Ordered on Vistaprint 250 per box cost average $19.00
- Use the shortened URL so the QR Code is easy to scan
- Our office orders the business cards and they are sent to author address

Extendable Banner, foam board, merchandise
Retractable banner or foam board are ordered from Vistaprint and sent to author address directly.

- Simple and easy to use
- Great for live events
- Average cost is $30
- Shipped directly to author's house

Square-up account
Square-up account is easy to set up and allows authors to sell books at live events or accept cards over the phone.

- Free to sign-up for the account
- Links directly to the bank account
- Small fee when credit cards are taken
- Download an app to use the account on the cell phone

Author recorded interview
The interview is 6-8 Minutes and will be uploaded to the Glorybound Publishing Youtube channel. URL is provided and is useful for websites and social media promotion of the author.

Bookstores and event sales
We can discuss options at varying bookstores and events considering wholesale vs retail sales.

Marketplace Website Advertisement

Web Advertising. It is important to have an on-line presence with the book. Any additional sites are added value to the promotion of the book.

- Book Clubs. Many book organizations provide a place to show a book and/or an author. Make use of those.
- Author website. Many authors have websites. We can assist to link their book to their website directly.
- Book Marketplace websites. Glorybound Publishing maintains several topic specific book marketing websites.

Book Marketplace
https://bookmarketplace.net A Central Hub for lots of books
https://brainebook.com Books to make you smart
https://awesomepoetry.shop Poetry
https://womensbooks.shop Women's books
https://Arizonabooks.shop Arizona Books
https://historybooks.shop History Books

Children's sites
https://animalbooks4kids.shop Animal books for children
https://Bookstore4kids.com Lots of books for children
https://homeschoolbooks.shop Homeschool books for children
https://dogandcatbooks.shop Dog and cat books for children

Christian Marketplace
https://godbookmarketplace.net A central hub for Christian Marketplace
https://christianwomensbooks.shop Christian Women's books
https://christianmensbooks.shop Christian Men's Books

Authors may put up to 3 books by one author on 2 sites for $10/month. Go to one of the hubs to sign up for the book marketplace https://bookmarketplace.net or https://godbookmarketplace.net

Amazon pay-per-click Ad
We build a custom pay-per-click ad on Amazon. The ad is based on keywords and projected sales.

- Average Amazon ad should run from 6-8 months
- Generally, begin at $300 per month allowance
- Can group books to advertise more than one at a time if they are linked
- E-book or paperback book

Book Market Mania Zoom Sessions

https://bookmarketmania.com

Providing a place for up-to-date book marketing education, sharing new books, and helping to establish valued book reviews

Live interactive zoom sessions 1.5 hr [see the calendar on the website for dates and times], led by publisher, Sheri Hauser.

After the book summary sharing, there will be a time for publishing and marketing questions.

Education related to current book marketing (15 min)

One or more authors sharing books while offering free copies to participants (15 min)

Each book shared will receive an editorial review by Glorybound Publishing on the website.

See the website for the current cost of the Book Mania Marketing Sessions.

To share a book during a Book Market Mania Session:

One book per author per session.

The title must be offered on Amazon during the sharing time period (5-days free on KENP, Kindle Edition Normalized Pages)

Book cover, summary, ISBN, price of book (all formats)

Must be a vetted member

The idea is that those participating in the Zoom will have an option to download the books, which are summarized by their respective authors and offer unbiased reviews.

Book Marketing Videos

ZAG Videos

Book Market Mania Zoom Author Group (ZAG) Providing a place for up-to-date book marketing education, sharing new books, and helping to establish valued book reviews.

ZAG 1 Making Your Book for Free on KDP

This video shows authors how to use a feature on KDP helps to promote sales by allowing the e-book to be offered free of charge for 5 days twice per year. Sheri Hauser walks through the process of making the book for free on the KDP website where your book is listed.

https://youtu.be/0AVToDmzIgM

ZAG 2 Registering a Book Title on KDP

This video walks through the steps of registering a title (to become a hardbound) book on KDP answering crucial questions related to filling in the blanks on the form. The video begins at the front of uploading a book and concludes at the point of actually uploading the book files to the website. See ZAG 2B Uploading a Book to KDP.

https://youtu.be/Wv4iLSdfLXg

ZAG 3 Uploading a Book to KDP

The video shows step by step the process of uploading a hard-bound book to the KDP website. It walks through uploading the files, the cover, verifying the book, recognizing the print price and entering the retail price. The video concludes with publishing a hard-bound title making it available on Amazon.

https://youtu.be/Fjh2uRTSd6E

ZAG 4 Locating Royalties on KDP

The video walks through the desktop of KDP (after a book is published) and shows how to figure out how much money a book is taking in. The video also covers locating where to obtain a tax royalty form from KDP for the amount earned on books sold for the year.

https://youtu.be/BDjbRso5KDg

ZAG 5 Author Central
The video shows how to get to Author Central from KDP desktop, where to upload a profile and photo and how to obtain a unique author URL from Author Central. It points out the benefits of registering for Author Central.
https://youtu.be/GbLBV7hHMg4

ZAG 6 **Driving your Book**
Sheri Hauser from Glorybound Publishing shares practical book marketing advice based on a dream metaphor about authors learning to "drive" their own books rather than waiting for external help. Key tips include checking and fixing your ebook on Amazon before releasing it for free promotions, finding effective keywords using tools like KDP Rocket, and creating a compelling third-of-a-page book summary. She emphasizes the importance of crafting meaningful book reviews, gathering supportive emails, and thinking beyond self-promotion by helping others. Promotional materials like an author sheet with interactive elements are crucial for visibility. Hauser also highlights the stages of book selling: announcing, releasing, offering free promotions, and following up with readers. She explains how to encourage genuine book reviews and the value of promoting your book on social media to connect it with interested readers.
https://youtu.be/SanCb8nmcvA

ZAG 7 Translating a Language Using AI Tools
In this video publisher Sheri Hauser walks through the process of translating a book which was originally written in Polish into English using two AI tools. There are several conversions needed. Acrobat, Word, IvoryMind and Quillbot are used. Enjoy the show!
https://youtu.be/1ppsqN2CbiQ

ZAG 8 Book Reviews Good, Better and Best

The video provides guidance on writing book reviews, categorizing them into good, better, and best reviews. The best reviews include a compelling opening statement, meaningful content showing the reviewer has read the book, and a personal connection to the material. It also explains how to leave a review on Amazon, find the book's URL, and create a QR code for easy access. Additionally, it notes that anyone who has purchased over $50 on Amazon can leave reviews, including unverified ones if they have not bought the book through Amazon, and offers caution about excessive unverified reviews. Finally, it mentions using Kindle promotions to make the book available twice a year for free.

https://youtu.be/rIfs70UcgCg

Contact the Author
sheri@gloryboundpublishing.com
www.gloryboundpublishing.com
www.sherihauser.com

www.ingramcontent.com/pod-product-compliance
Lightning Source LLC
LaVergne TN
LVHW030922080826
845145LV00013B/3012

* 9 7 8 1 6 0 7 8 9 2 6 9 4 *